THE INTERNATIONAL JOURNAL OF ETHICAL LEADERSHIP

Volume 5
Fall 2018

CASE WESTERN RESERVE UNIVERSITY | INAMORI INTERNATIONAL CENTER FOR ETHICS AND EXCELLENCE

The International Journal of Ethical Leadership
Case Western Reserve University
Editor-in-Chief: Shannon E. French, Inamori Professor in Ethics and
   Director, Inamori International Center for Ethics and Excellence
Executive Editor: Michael Scharf, Dean of the School of Law, John
   Deaver Drinko-Baker & Hostetler Professor of Law, and Director,
   Frederick K. Cox International Law Center
Managing Editor: Laura Mekhail, Inamori International Center for
   Ethics and Excellence

The International Journal of Ethical Leadership, Volume 5, Fall 2018

All new material © 2018 *The International Journal of Ethical Leadership*.

All rights reserved • Manufactured in the United States of America

ISSN 2326-7461

For additional information, please contact Editor-in-Chief Shannon E. French,
sef37@case.edu or visit case.edu/provost/inamori

Contents

Message from the Editor

Shannon E. French
Inamori Professor in Ethics and Director,
Inamori International Center for Ethics and Excellence,
Case Western Reserve University

The first Inamori Ethics Prize for outstanding ethical leadership on the global stage was presented at Case Western Reserve University in 2008 to Francis Collins, leader of the Human Genome Project (and current director of the NIH). For our tenth anniversary celebration of the prize in September 2018, we will be honoring another great American scientist: Farouk El-Baz. As a geologist, Egyptian-born El-Baz played a central role in the NASA Apollo space missions, including helping to select the first lunar landing site. He educated the Apollo astronauts about what they would find on the moon and encouraged them to see all of their efforts as being done not only for the United States, but also for all of humankind. After retiring from NASA, El-Baz dedicated himself to using the skills he learned as part of the team exploring space to explore the Earth, searching for desperately needed resources. He created and still directs a NASA-recognized "Center of Excellence" at Boston University: the Center for Remote Sensing. The center uses space technology to study the Earth and its environment, including finding critically needed groundwater in arid regions around the globe to bring water resources to the people, and help resolve water-based conflicts in places like Darfur.

Farouk El-Baz joins an impressive cohort of Inamori Ethics Prize recipients who have shown us what ethical leadership looks like in a wide variety of fields:

- **2017: Marian Wright Edelman**
  For decades, Marian Wright Edelman has been an advocate for children's rights and the disadvantaged. Under her leadership, the nonprofit Children's Defense Fund, which Edelman established in 1973, has become the nation's leading advocacy organization for children and families, championing policies and programs to lift children from poverty, protect them from abuse and neglect, and ensure their access to healthcare and high-quality education.

Edelman, a graduate of Spelman College and Yale Law School, began her career in the mid-1960s when, as the first black woman admitted to the Mississippi Bar, directed the NAACP Legal Defense and Educational Fund office in Jackson, Mississippi. She has received more than 100 honorary degrees and numerous awards, including the Albert Schweitzer Humanitarian Prize, the Heinz Award, and a MacArthur Foundation Prize Fellowship. In 2000, she received the Presidential Medal of Freedom—the US's highest civilian award—and the Robert F. Kennedy Lifetime Achievement Award, for her writings.

- **2016: Peter Eigen**
  A pioneer of the global fight against corruption, Peter Eigen has developed and led groundbreaking initiatives to improve governance and raise awareness of corruption's devastating effects on economic growth, social welfare, and justice. A lawyer by training, he has worked in economic development for several decades, investigating how abuses of power can undermine the public's trust and cost people their freedom, health, money, and, sometimes, their lives.
  Following positions with the World Bank in Latin America and Africa, Eigen founded Transparency International (TI) in 1993. With chapters in more than one hundred nations, TI has become the leading nongovernmental organization promoting transparency and accountability in development. TI collaborates with governments, businesses, and citizens to stop the abuse of power, bribery, and secret deals. The organization's impact spans the public sector and industries ranging from finance to oil to sport.

- **2015: Martha C. Nussbaum**
  Martha C. Nussbaum is an American philosopher and one of the world's leading intellectuals, particularly on issues of moral and political theory, education, social equality, emotions, feminism, and ancient Greek and Roman philosophy. She is the Ernst Freund Distinguished Service Professor of Law and Ethics at the University of Chicago, with appointments in the philosophy department and the law school.

Nussbaum's work has been at the forefront of some of the most salient contemporary ethical issues. Alongside economist Amartya Sen, she reoriented conversations of international welfare efforts away from exclusive focus on gross domestic product and toward the capabilities of a nation's individuals. Nussbaum is a founding president of the Human Development and Capability Association, and she has received prizes and fifty-one honorary degrees from institutions across the globe. In 2016, Nussbaum was awarded the prestigious Kyoto Prize in Arts and Philosophy.

- **2014: Denis Mukwege**
  A deeply committed physician and human rights activist, Denis Mukwege has worked tirelessly with and for women who have suffered excruciatingly traumatic and violent attacks in the name of war. The Panzi Hospital, which he founded in war-torn Bukavu, Congo, and where he serves as manager and chief surgeon, is known worldwide for its treatment of women with severe gynecological problems, predominantly the result of sexual violence. Panzi has become a beacon of hope for thousands of women, including those who cannot afford treatment, for whom it is free.
  Mukwege has persisted in his mission, despite threats and attacks on his life. As a result of his perseverance, he and his hospital colleagues had treated more than forty thousand rape survivors as of the time of his receiving the Inamori Ethics Prize. A longtime outspoken advocate for gender equality and women's rights, he has been recognized by many organizations and institutions for both his medical knowledge and his commitment to ending sexual violence in the Democratic Republic of Congo, including having been nominated three times for the Nobel Peace Prize (2009, 2013, and 2018).

- **2013: Yvon Chouinard**
  The founder of the outdoor clothing and gear company Patagonia, Inc., Yvon Chouinard is one of the most successful and ethical outdoor industry executives alive today. Chouinard is considered a trailblazer and leader in ecologically responsible corporate operations, to which philosophy he steadfastly adheres

even when it is at the expense of Patagonia's bottom line. Chouinard's driving objective is to protect the environment, and he has continually demonstrated that this mission does not have to be at odds with a highly successful business. From launching the organic cotton industry in California because of traditional cotton's terrible environmental impact to giving Patagonia employees financial incentives to work on local environmental projects, Chouinard has for decades demonstrated an active, unwavering commitment to prioritizing the environment while maintaining—and growing—a flourishing corporation. Distinguished journalist and author Tom Brokaw said of Chouinard, "He walks the walk more than anyone else I know in American business."

- **2012: David Suzuki**
  Passionate environmentalist and broadcaster David Suzuki is a global leader on issues of sustainable ecology and climate justice. Esteemed around the world for his radio and television programs, documentaries, and publications, Suzuki is a powerful voice for biodiversity, future generations, and the planet. A celebrated academic, Suzuki earned his PhD in zoology from the University of Chicago. He worked for over 40 years as a professor in genetics and at the University of British Columbia's Sustainable Research Development Institute, where he is now professor emeritus.
  In 1990, Suzuki co-founded the David Suzuki Foundation whose main missions are transforming the economy, protecting the climate, reconnecting with nature, and building communities of individuals who live healthier, more fulfilled, and just lives.

- **2011: Beatrice Mtetwa**
  Human rights lawyer Beatrice Mtetwa has spent over twenty-five years defending journalists and resisting government corruption in her home country of Zimbabwe. Born and educated in Swaziland, Mtetwa was the first member of her family to graduate from college. After earning her law degree, she worked as a prosecutor in Swaziland before moving to Zimbabwe,

where her career focus began to shift to family law and human rights.

In her two decades defending domestic journalists, foreign correspondents and victims of human rights violations against Zimbabwe's restrictive government, Mtetwa has been physically attacked and faced threats against her life. Yet despite such adversity, she continues to fight for freedom and the ideals of democracy. In addition to journalists' rights, Mtetwa champions a variety of other social causes, including eradicating AIDS and poverty, protecting the rights of women and children, preserving the essential freedoms of peaceful assembly, association and speech, and helping poor farmers wrongfully evicted from their land by the government.

- **2010: Stan Brock**
  Stan Brock's nonprofit organization Remote Area Medical (RAM) delivers free healthcare services to underserved communities in the United States and isolated regions around the world. A humanitarian, conservationist, and former co-host of the TV show *Wild Kingdom*, Brock founded RAM in 1985. Staffed by volunteer doctors, dentists, nurses, and veterinarians, RAM has served hundreds of thousands of patients at its mobile free clinics. RAM conducts these medical missions wherever they are needed, regardless of danger or difficult conditions—from the hills of Appalachia near its home base in Tennessee to the mountains of Nepal. Brock himself draws virtually no salary from RAM and lives frugally, devoting his time and energy exclusively to RAM's mission.

- **2009: Mary Robinson**
  The former United Nations High Commissioner on Human Rights, Mary Robinson was the second honoree of the Inamori Prize. Noted for her work as an advocate for global human rights, health care, sustainability, and corporate responsibility, Robinson was instrumental in changing the face of Anglo-Irish relations when she was Ireland's first woman president. She is one of twelve world leaders who make up The Elders—an organization formed by Nelson Mandela to contribute wisdom,

independent leadership, and integrity to tackling some of the world's greatest challenges. She founded the nonprofit organization Realizing Rights: The Ethical Globalization Initiative, which promotes equitable trade, humane practices in the work environment, corporate responsibility, and women's leadership. She has recently been a professor of practice in international affairs at Columbia University, chair of the Gavi Alliance Board to improve children's health around the world, the honorary president of Oxfam International, and honorary chair of the LIVESTRONG Global Cancer Summit.

- **2008: Francis S. Collins**
  The inaugural Inamori Ethics Prize was awarded in 2008 to physician-geneticist Francis S. Collins, who was recognized for his principled leadership of the Human Genome Project. Collins understood the project's potential for improvement of humankind and fought for those benefits to be shared around the world and not kept secret or controlled by for-profit entities. Noted for his landmark discoveries of disease genes, Collins served as the National Human Genome Research Institute Director at the National Institutes for Health, where his laboratory is dedicated to researching rare and common gene-related diseases. His laboratory has discovered genes responsible for cystic fibrosis, neurofibrosis, Huntington's disease, adult-onset diabetes, and Hutchinson–Gilford syndrome. In 2009, he became the sixteenth director of the National Institutes of Health (NIH).

The Inamori Ethics Prize celebrates and illustrates ethical leadership in all its forms, across a range of human endeavors. We look forward to getting to know the next decade of prize recipients. The process for selecting the prize recipients is quite extensive. Each year, we consider about one hundred nominated candidates for the prize. Researchers at the Inamori Center create short biographies of the candidates, highlighting their accomplishments and the challenges they have overcome. Three committees then intensively review the candidates: the Inamori Center Advisory Board, the Inamori Center Faculty and Staff Affiliates Council, and the Ethics Alliance. When the finalists emerge, they are further reviewed by an ad hoc Executive Committee and research librarians from Case Western Reserve

University's Kelvin Smith Library. A final report is then presented to the university President and Provost, who select the recipient from among the committee's approved finalists. If you would like to nominate someone for the Inamori Ethics Prize, please do so via our website at: https://case.edu /events/featured-events/inamori-ethics-prize/inamori-ethics-prize -nomination-form

We hope you will enjoy this issue of the *International Journal of Ethical Leadership,* which we dedicate to the recipients, past and future, of the Inamori Ethics Prize. Dr. Kazuo Inamori, whose philosophy underlies and inspires our mission of ethical engagement at the Inamori International Center for Ethics and Excellence, has sagely observed, "Human beings have no higher calling than to serve the greater good of humankind and society." The Inamori Ethics Prize recipients live up to this ideal and remind us that we all have the capacity to show ethical leadership in everything that we do.

The State of America's Children

Marian Wright Edelman
Children's Defense Fund

It is a great honor to receive the 2017 Inamori Ethics Prize from the Inamori International Center for Ethics and Excellence at Case Western Reserve University enabled by the Inamori Foundation. Your mission of fostering ethical leadership locally, nationally and globally is crucial in these turbulent times.

We are living at an incredible magical moment in history—blessed to experience the beginning of both a new century and millennium. How will we say thanks for the life, earth, nation, and children God has entrusted to our care? What legacies and values will we stand for and send to the future through our children to their children and to a spiritually confused, balkanized, and violent world desperately hungering for moral leadership, peace, justice and community?

How will progress be measured over the next ten, hundred, and thousand years if we survive them? By the kill power and number of weapons of destruction we can produce, or by our willingness to shrink, indeed destroy, the global prison of violence constructed in the name of peace and security? Will our era be remembered by how many material things we can manufacture, advertise, sell, and consume, or by our rediscovery of more lasting, nonmaterial measures of success—a new Dow Jones for the quality of life and justice in our families, national, and world communities? Will our legacy be how rapidly technology and corporate mergermania and greed can render human beings obsolete or by our efforts to reach a better balance between corporate profits, and corporate caring for families, children, communities, and the environment? Will we be remembered by how much a very few at the top can get at the expense of the many at the bottom and in the middle or by our determination to close the huge gap between the haves and have-nots in a world where the world's eight wealthiest people (all billionaires) own the same combined wealth as the 3.6 billion people who make up the world's population.

Something is awry in our own great nation when the richest one percent of Americans own about as much wealth as the bottom ninety percent of America combined; when the 400 highest-income taxpayers earned as much as the combined tax revenue of twenty-two states and the District of Columbia in 2014; when the highest-paid American CEO took home over $94 million in 2016, more than the combined average annual salaries of 4,240 child care workers; and when the gap between rich and poor has reached historic heights not seen since the 1920s.

Dietrich Bonhoeffer, the German Protestant theologian who died opposing Hitler's holocaust, said the test of the morality of a society is how it treats its children. The United States is failing Bonhoeffer's test daily by permitting a child to be abused or neglected every forty-seven seconds; (to be) born into poverty every forty-eight seconds; (to be) born without health insurance every sixty seconds; and (to be) killed by guns every three hours and eight minutes. We have lost nearly 180,000 children to gunfire in America since 1963. A child is killed or injured by a gun every thirty-two minutes and we are standing for it. Between 1963 and 2015, nearly 65,000 Black children and teens have been killed by guns—more than fifteen times the recorded lynchings of Black people of all ages in the seventy-four years from 1877 to 1950.

These facts are not acts of God. They are our choices as human beings. We can and must change them.

Albert Camus, speaking at a Dominican Monastery in 1948 said: "Perhaps we cannot prevent this world from being a world in which children are tortured. But we can reduce the number of tortured children." He described our responsibility as human beings "if not to reduce evil, at least not to add to it" and "to refuse to consent to conditions which torture innocents." "I continue," he said "to struggle against this universe in which children suffer and die." And so must every one of us. Only then will the cries of the prophets for justice and peace become a lasting reality.

The day Dr. King was assassinated, he called his mother to give her his next Sunday's sermon title: "Why America May Go to Hell." He warned that "America is going to hell if we don't use her vast resources to end poverty and make it possible for all of God's children to have the basic necessities of life." It is a national moral disgrace that there are more than 13.2 million poor children in the United States—one of the world's richest nations. It is also unnecessary, costly and the greatest threat I believe to our future national, economic and military security and national soul.

The younger children are, the poorer they are during their years of greatest brain development. Every other American baby is nonwhite and nearly one in two Black babies is poor, 150 years after slavery was legally abolished.

The Children's Defense Fund commissioned the Urban Institute to analyze nine policies for their poverty alleviation impact. We released a 2015 report, which we are updating now, calling for an end to child poverty right now in the richest nation on earth. Our report showed that solutions to ending child poverty in our nation already exist and for the first time showed how, by expanding investments in nine existing programs that work, we could shrink overall child poverty sixty percent, Black child poverty seventy-two percent, and improve economic circumstances for ninety-seven percent of poor children at a cost of $77.2 billion a year. These policies could be implemented immediately, improving the lives and futures of millions of children and eventually saving taxpayers hundreds of billions of dollars annually.

America's poor children did not ask to be born; did not choose their parents, country, state, neighborhood, race, color, or faith. In fact, at the time of the report if they had been born in thirty-four other Organization for Economic Cooperation and Development (OECD) countries they would be less likely to be poor. Among these thirty-five countries, America ranked thirty-fourth in relative child poverty—ahead only of Romania whose economy is ninety-nine percent smaller than ours.

The United Kingdom committed to and succeeded in cutting its child poverty rate by half in ten years. It is about values and political will. Sadly, politics too often trumps good policy, moral decency, and responsibility to the next generation and the nation's future. It is way past time for a critical mass of Americans to confront the hypocrisy of America's pretension to be a fair playing field while more than 13.2 million children languish in poverty we have the capacity—but not the will—to prevent and alleviate.

Child poverty is too expensive to continue. Every year we keep these millions of children in poverty costs our nation about $500 billion—six times more than the $77 billion investment we proposed to reduce child poverty by sixty percent. MIT Nobel Laureate economist and 2014 Presidential Medal of Freedom recipient Dr. Robert Solow in his foreword to a 1994 CDF report *Wasting America's Future* presciently wrote:

> "For many years Americans have allowed child poverty levels to remain astonishingly high...far higher than one would think a rich and ethical society would tolerate. The justification, when one is offered at all, has often been that action is expensive: 'We have more will than wallet.' I suspect that in fact our wallets exceed our will, but in any event this concern for the drain on

our resources completely misses the other side of the equation: Inaction has its costs too....As an economist I believe that good things are worth paying for; and that even if curing children's poverty were expensive, it would be hard to think of a better use in the world for money. If society cares about children, it should be willing to spend money on them."

Not only does child poverty cost far more than eliminating it would, we have so many better choices that reflect more just values as well as economic savings. I believe that food, shelter, quality early childhood investments to get every child ready for school and an equitable education for all children should take precedence over massive welfare for the rich and blatantly excessive spending for military weapons that often do not work.

We can afford to act now to establish a floor of economic decency for all our children if our leaders think that we can afford more tax breaks for millionaires and billionaires. In our 2015 report we identified a few ways to fund the $77 billion—two percent of our national budget—that at the time was necessary to make a huge down payment on ending preventable, costly and immoral child poverty in our wealthy nation.

- Closing tax loopholes that let U.S. corporations avoid $90 billion in federal income taxes each year by shifting profits to subsidiaries in tax havens.

or

- Eliminating tax breaks for the wealthy by taxing capital gains and dividends at the same rates as wages, saving more than $84 billion a year.

or

- Closing twenty-three tax loopholes that at the time were in House Ways and Means Chairman Dave Camp's Tax Reform Act of 2014 which would have freed up an average of $79.3 billion a year.

or

- Decreasing fourteen percent of the nation's FY2015 $578 million military budget. The U.S. has less than five percent of the world's population but thirty-seven percent of the world's military expenditures.

or

- Scrapping the F-35 fighter jet program which was several years behind schedule and sixty-eight percent over budget and still not producing fully functional planes. For the nearly $400 billion projected costs of this program, the nation could reduce child poverty by sixty percent for five years.

If we love America and love our children we must all stand against the excessive greed that tramples millions of our children entrusted to our care. America's Declaration of Independence says, "We hold these truths to be self-evident, that all men are created equal, and are endowed by their creator with certain inalienable rights." After more than two centuries, it is time to make those truths evident in the lives of all poor children and to close our intolerable national hypocrisy gap and show the world whether democratic capitalism is an oxymoron or can work. A nation that does not stand for children does not stand for anything and will not stand tall in the twenty-first century world or before God.

Let me end with a few lessons from Noah's Ark according to an anonymous sage in an old clipping that appeared in my home mail some years ago and a few examples of how one determined person can make a difference:

Lesson One: Don't miss the boat. The United States is going to miss the boat to lead and compete in our globalizing world because we are not preparing millions of our children for the future—especially nonwhite children who soon will be a majority of our child population. More than sixty percent of all public school fourth and eighth graders and almost seventy-five percent of Latino and Black students in these grades cannot read or compute at grade level and dropout rates are rampant; about seventy-one percent of seventeen to twenty-four-year olds would fail to qualify if they applied for military service because of reasons related to health, criminal records and drug abuse, literacy, and other education problems.

Lesson Two: We are all in the same boat. Many Americans may not like or think they have any self interest in assuring a fair playing field for other people's children—especially poor and nonwhite children who by 2020 will constitute a majority of our child population and future workers. But isn't it better to prepare them to be a productive workforce than for us to support them in costly prisons where they increase neither our safety nor our productivity? Yet the U.S. spends more than twice as much per prisoner than per public school pupil. [Note: 2011–2012 data shows Ohio was second-best, at 1.8 only behind Vermont]. I can't think of a dumber investment policy.

Lesson Three: Plan ahead. It wasn't raining when Noah built the Ark. Tomorrow is today and children have only one childhood. Providing *all* children a healthy start, quality early childhood experiences, first rate schools with first rate caring teachers who have high expectations for every child, and stimulating high quality out of school time programs must be the first order of national, state and community business in our quick fix, quarterly profit driven culture. And we must build a strong nonwhite teacher pipeline to better reflect the demographics of our child and public school population. Black, Brown and other nonwhite children since the 2014–2015 school year have been the majority of our public school population. They should be able to see themselves and their cultures reflected in the leadership, books and pedagogy of their schools.

Lesson Four: Don't listen to critics and naysayers. If you don't want to be criticized, don't say anything, do anything, or be anything.

Lesson Five: For safety's sake, travel in pairs and—better still—in community groups and coalitions. Lone ranger and top down leadership will not work. We must together reweave the fabric of family and community and utilize the power of our individual and collective voices and votes with urgency and persistence for children and the poor. Sprinters, dabblers and press hogs are not welcome. We need marathon runners and servant leaders—not self-serving leaders.

Lesson Six—my favorite: Remember that the Ark was built by amateurs; the Titanic by experts. Too many of us are waiting for Dr. King to come back. He's gone. Use your citizen power and vote to wrest our ship of state from experts and powerful special interests who too often recklessly jeopardize all of our lives and our children's futures for personal gain and take more than their fair share of our nation's wealth and income.

Let's build our nation's future on higher ground and leave it better than we found it—more just, more hopeful, more peaceful, more productive, inclusive and unified. This may be the first time in our history when our children and grandchildren will be worse off than their parents and grandparents unless we correct course and do whatever is necessary to get them to safe harbor. God did not make two classes of children and we continue to do so at our soul and nation and world's peril.

What can each of us do to honor the spirit of this Inamori Ethics prize?

1. Avoid convenient ignorance—refusing to see the obvious suffering and unjust governmental and private sector policies in plain sight if our eyes were not deliberately closed or diverted.

2. If you do see, don't ask why doesn't somebody do something about child hunger, gun deaths, homelessness, unjust treatment and unequal school funding in schools and other institutions for poor and nonwhite or disabled children. [Public education in America and Ohio is still separate and unequal if you are a child of color or poor.] And we must all see and break up the Cradle to Prison Pipeline™ which continues to trap thousands upon thousands of Black, Latino and Native American boys. Incarceration for profit is a huge industry in America which must be stopped now.

3. Persist—democracy is not a spectator sport and one-day advocates or once in a while citizen participants let's our country and world down. The German playwright Bertolt Brecht wrote: "There are those who struggle for a day and they are good. There are those who struggle for a year and they are better. There are those who struggle all their lives. These are the indispensable ones." Be an indispensable one.

4. Let's accept our responsibility to pass onto our children and grandchildren a safer and better world than we inherited.

5. Struggle to be an ethical human being who simply refuses to stop demanding justice for all children. God did not make two classes of children.

Two of my lifelong role models are Sojourner Truth and Harriet Tubman—both slave women who were determined to free themselves and others from slavery. One day Sojourner Truth was heckled by a White man in the audience who asserted he didn't care any more about her antislavery talk than a flea bite. She replied "[That's alright] but, the Lord willing, I'll keep you scratching." We don't have to be big dogs trying to make big differences or big headlines. Working together with others strategically biting and voting as fleas, we can make the biggest dogs uncomfortable.

Harriet Tubman escaped slavery and created an underground railroad to the North and freedom and returned again and again to free slaves left behind. She boasted that she never lost a passenger. I can't think of any airline, train or bus company that can match her record.

As we approach the fiftieth anniversary of Dr. King's call for a campaign to end poverty in wealthy America, I hope we will make a down payment in 2018 by committing to ending child poverty now for which we will be issuing a call soon—working in coalition with others—and issuing a new report and outlined goals. I hope you will join us in moving Dr. King's dream forward and stop the attempts of many of our political leaders to destroy the laboriously woven safety net over the past fifty years that has helped millions of children avoid hunger; enabled ninety percent of children to get health coverage with the help of thanks to Medicaid and CHIP and the Affordable Care Act; millions of children to get a Head Start and lay the foundation for a long overdue and not yet completed high quality early childhood system to prepare every child for school and success in life. We must go forward as Dr. King told me and other Spelman College students in chapel in 1960—never backwards. "If you can't fly," he said, "drive. If you can't drive, run. If you can't run, walk. If you can't walk, crawl. But always go forward." Let us honor and heed his call and build a fairer and safer America in a world hungry for moral leadership, justice and peace.

Where Are They Now
Ten Years of Past Inamori Prize Winners

Francis S. Collins, 2008 Inamori Ethics Prize Recipient
Ellen Kendall

At the turn of the century, an international research group led by Francis S. Collins, successfully sequenced the three million DNA base pairs that make up the human genome, providing the global community a first look at the code that makes up human life. The success of the Human Genome Project, completed in 2003, has allowed researchers to learn more about hereditary influences of diseases like cancer and diabetes. The long-term impact of the Human Genome Project has exponential potential as researchers are just beginning to translate the information from the genetic code into tangible solutions for patients, leading to earlier detection of illness, new therapeutic interventions, and ultimately cures that can save lives.[1]

The revolutionary Human Genome Project was led by a biomedical scientist, Francis Collins. Collins is a physician-geneticist who, early in his career, developed innovative methods to isolate genes responsible in diseases such as cystic fibrosis and Huntington's disease. Collins became the director of the National Human Genome Research Institute (NHGRI) in 1993, where he oversaw large initiatives such as the Human Genome Project and the HapMap Project, which mapped common human genetic variation.[2] Collins stepped down as the director of the NHGRI in 2008, and in 2009, was appointed by President Barack Obama to become the director of the National Institutes of Health (NIH). Collins remains the active director of the NIH after being reappointed by President Donald Trump in 2017.[3]

As the director of the NIH, Collins oversees the largest supporter of biomedical research in the world. During his tenure, Collins has helped to found the National Center for Advancing Translational Sciences,[4] the Brain Research through Advancing Innovative Neurotechnologies Project,[5] and the Precision Medicine Initiative,[6] while simultaneously running his own lab at the NIH in the Medical Genomics and Metabolic Genetics Branch.[7] The landmark discoveries and scientific leadership of Collins have earned him prestigious recognitions such as his elections to the National Academy of Medicine and the National Academy of Science, his awarding of the

Presidential Medal of Freedom in November 2007, and his selection as the recipient of the National Medal of Science in 2009.

In addition to his scientific achievements, Collins has led the biomedical research community by example with his commitment to ethical and legal issues. Collins worked to protect the privacy of genetic information by helping to pass the Genetic Information and Nondiscrimination Act,[8] helped expand genetic research in Africa with the Human Heredity and Health in Africa (H3Africa) Project,[9] and helped shape controversial national policies on allowing the use of embryonic stem cells in research[10] and banning the use of chimpanzees in NIH-funded research.[11] Collins was awarded the inaugural Inamori Ethics Prize in 2008 for his commitment to ethical leadership and scientific achievements.[12]

Francis Collins is a revolutionary researcher, a humane scientist, and a charismatic leader. He has worked tirelessly to turn his discoveries into cures, and he is deeply committed to using his scientific discoveries for good in the world. Now, as the director of the NIH, he is leading other scientists to do the same.

Notes

1. "What Was the Human Genome Project and Why Has It Been Important?–Genetics Home Reference." U.S. National Library of Medicine, National Institutes of Health, Apr. 17, 2018, ghr.nlm.nih.gov/primer/hgp/description.
2. "Former NHGRI Director Francis Collins' Biography." National Human Genome Research Institute (NHGRI), National Institutes of Health, www.genome.gov/10001018/former-nhgri-director-francis-collins-biography/.
3. "Biographical Sketch of Francis S. Collins, MD, PhD" National Institutes of Health, U.S. Department of Health and Human Services, June 27, 2017, www.nih.gov/about-nih/who-we-are/nih-director/biographical-sketch-francis-s-collins-md-phd.
4. "About the Center." National Center for Advancing Translational Sciences, U.S. Department of Health and Human Services, Apr. 20, 2018, ncats.nih.gov/about/center.
5. "About Us–Brain Research through Advancing Innovative Neurotechnologies (BRAIN)." National Institutes of Health, U.S. Department of Health and Human Services, www.braininitiative.nih.gov/about/index.htm.
6. "What Is the Precision Medicine Initiative?–Genetics Home Reference." U.S. National Library of Medicine, National Institutes of Health, Apr. 2015, ghr.nlm.nih.gov/primer/precisionmedicine/initiative.
7. "Principal Investigators." National Institutes of Health, U.S. Department of Health and Human Services, irp.nih.gov/pi/francis-collins.
8. "S.1053–108th Congress (2003–2004): Genetic Information Nondiscrimination Act of 2003." Congress.gov, Oct. 15, 2003, www.congress.gov/bill/108th-congress/senate-bill/1053.
9. "Funding Agencies." H3Africa, h3africa.org/about/people.
10. "Embryonic Stem Cells, Francis Collins, and the NIH." The Lancet, vol. 374, no. 9685, 2009, p. 175., doi: 10.1016/s0140-6736(09)61308-8.
11. "NIH Will No Longer Support Biomedical Research on Chimpanzees." National Institutes of Health, U.S. Department of Health and Human Services, Nov. 19, 2015,

www.nih.gov/about-nih/who-we-are/nih-director/statements/nih-will-no-longer
-support-biomedical-research-chimpanzees.
12. "NHGRI Director to Receive International Ethics Prize." National Human Genome
Research Institute (NHGRI), Oct. 30, 2010, www.genome.gov/26525767/nhgri-director
-to-receive-international-ethics-prize/.

Mary Robinson, 2009 Inamori Ethics Prize Recipient
Jacob Sandstrom

In September 2009, Mary Robinson became the second recipient of the Inamori Ethics Prize at Case Western Reserve University, one month after being awarded the Presidential Medal of Freedom by former U.S. President Barack Obama.[1] The first female president of Ireland from 1990 to 1997, Robinson is a stalwart supporter of freedom, a crusader for human rights, and a pioneer in advocating for conscientious action on climate change. In addition to her tenure as president of Ireland, Robinson served as the United Nations High Commissioner for Human Rights from 1997 to 2002, is the founder of the Mary Robinson Foundation–Climate Justice, and is an active member of The Elders, among many other notable achievements and accolades.

Since receiving the Inamori Ethics Prize, Mary Robinson has remained active in world affairs, speaking at multiple summits and working to resolve conflicts worldwide by advocating for peace, justice, and sustainability. Reflecting on her time as High Commissioner for Human Rights in 2013, Robinson noted that it is "important to have the stamina to work on something until it comes right."[2] Though no longer the High Commissioner, Robinson has been involved with the United Nations and has used her stamina to spark key dialogues on issues of conflict resolution and climate. A well-respected world leader, Mary Robinson continues to use her prominence as a force for positive change.

United Nations Secretary-General Ban Ki-moon appointed Mary Robinson as the one-year Special Envoy for the Great Lakes Region of Africa to support "implementation of the Peace Security and Cooperation for the Democratic Republic of the Congo" in 2013.[3] In this role, Robinson called for increased support for implementing "all commitments at the national and regional levels" to ensure "concrete peace dividends and lasting life improvements to the people in the region."[4] While the Democratic Republic of the Congo remains rife with conflict, Mary Robinson's efforts made a marked difference.

Secretary-General Ban Ki-moon again called on Robinson to serve as his Special Envoy in 2014, this time to address climate change. As the Special Envoy for Climate Change, Robinson was charged with "engag[ing] Heads of State and Governments around the world in order to mobilize political will and action, and to raise ambition in advance of the 2014 Climate Summit."[5] Her exceptional work landed her yet another appointment to serve as a Special Envoy on El Niño and Climate in 2016, where she worked to address the threat of extreme weather in impoverished countries, particularly in East Africa, Southern Africa, Central America, and the Pacific.[6]

Beyond her official capacities at the United Nations, Robinson has worked closely with former U.S. President Jimmy Carter, Nelson Mandela, and other Elders, notably on de-escalation of the Korean Peninsula, Middle East peace, and climate change by engaging with aspirant young leaders and global citizens.[7] Her participation in important dialogues with former, current, and future leaders has led to the incorporation of human rights commitments in important global decisions, including the Paris Agreement.[8] She has also been vocal on issues of child marriage and the current refugee crisis.[9]

Mary Robinson's commitment to advocacy is driven by a desire to help people in the greatest need of support. In creating and maintaining the Mary Robinson Foundation–Climate Justice, Robinson has created a "platform for solidarity, partnership and shared engagement for all who care about global justice" that seeks to foster a "people-centered, developmental approach" to climate justice.[10] As the organization moves toward its 2020 goals, Robinson continues to forge her legacy as an effective, impressive, dedicated leader in many facets.

Robinson's vision and resolve continue to make a difference in global affairs, and despite setbacks, her outlook is positive. In 2017, Robinson expressed to *The Irish Times* that "she has become more optimistic about the global response to climate change" and encourages a "Marshall Plan" on climate based on increased knowledge and understanding.[11] Moving forward, Robinson intends to continue "to work for climate justice for so long as [she has] health and energy."[12]

Notes

1. "Presidential Medal of Freedom." CBS News. August 12, 2009. Accessed April 19, 2018. https://www.cbsnews.com/pictures/presidential-medal-of-freedom/10/.
2. Alison Beard, "Interview with Mary Robinson." *Harvard Business Review*. March 2013. Accessed April 19, 2018. https://hbr.org/2013/03/mary-robinson.
3. "Secretary-General Appoints Mary Robinson of Ireland Special Envoy for Great Lakes Region of Africa." United Nations. March 18, 2013. Accessed April 19, 2018. https://www.un.org/press/en/2013/sga1394.doc.htm.
4. "DR Congo Peace Efforts, Regional Framework at Crucial Juncture, UN Officials Stress." United Nations News. January 13, 2014. Accessed April 19, 2018. https://news.un.org/en/story/2014/01/459592-dr-congo-peace-efforts-regional-framework-crucial-juncture-un-officials-stress.

5. "Secretary-General Appoints Mary Robinson of Ireland Special Envoy for Climate Change." United Nations. July 14, 2014. Accessed April 19, 2018. https://www.un.org/press/en/2014/sga1481.doc.htm.
6. "Secretary-General Appoints Mary Robinson of Ireland, Macharia Kamau of Kenya Special Envoys on El Niño and Climate." United Nations. May 20, 2016. Accessed April 19, 2018. https://www.un.org/press/en/2016/sga1660.doc.htm.
7. "Profile: Mary Robinson." The Elders. Accessed April 19, 2018. https://www.theelders .org/mary-robinson.
8. "Profile: Mary Robinson."
9. "Profile: Mary Robinson."
10. "Mission and Vision." Mary Robinson Foundation–Climate Justice. Accessed April 19, 2018. https://www.mrfcj.org/about/mission-and-vision/.
11. Kevin O'Sullivan, "'Marshall Plan' Needed for Climate Change, Says Mary Robinson." *Irish Times*. November 14, 2017. Accessed April 19, 2018. https://www.irishtimes.com/news/environment/marshall-plan-needed-for-climate-change-says-mary-robinson -1.3291484.
12. Sheila Langan, "What Are You Like?: Mary Robinson." *Irish America Magazine*. June 2016. Accessed April 19, 2018. http://irishamerica.com/2016/06/what-are-you-like -mary-robinson-2/.

Stan Brock, 2010 Inamori Ethics Prize Recipient
Vanitha Raguveer

The 2010 recipient of the Inamori Ethics Prize, Stan Brock, remains a force of ethical leadership and profound service, bringing medical care directly to the people who need it most. Inspired by his own injury when overseeing the world's largest cattle ranch operation in Guyana, Brock went on to found Remote Area Medical (RAM) in 1985, which connects volunteer health professionals to rural communities that do not have adequate access to medical care. In 2016, RAM provided care to thirty-one thousand patients at seventy clinics, spending under $3 million, or $94 per encounter.[1] Since its founding, RAM has given more than $120 million in free medical care to almost one million men, women, and children. He also acted as an integral part of the passing of the Tennessee Volunteer Medical Services Act of 1995, which allows out-of-state health professionals to come to the area and provide free care to the community. Since then, ten more states have passed similar laws, allowing for more charity care to be provided. He has written three books: *Leemo, A True Story of a Man's Friendship with a Mountain Lion, More about Leemo,* and *Jungle Cowboy,* and has starred in two films, *Escape from Angola* and *Gaylon the Indestructible Man.*[2]

In 2012, Stan Brock was named a CNN Hero for the work he has pioneered, starting and running the largest free medical service provider in the U.S., but insisted that the volunteers were the true heroes, saying "All I do is show up and carry some of the luggage." On July 4, 2017, he received the 2017 Lions Humanitarian Award from the Lions International Foundation. This award, won by other prominent leaders like Mother Teresa and President Jimmy Carter, includes a $250,000 grant to continue on humanitarian activities, and represents an immense honor. With RAM's current clinics all around the U.S., Brock now hopes to expand the free clinics back to his homeland, Britain. Following his recent visit to investigate the state of dental care after changes to the National Health System, Brock recognized the public need for access to dental care and hopes to address this need.[3]

Under Brock's direction, RAM has set up clinics in various rural communities in states like Tennessee, Virginia, West Virginia, New York, Oklahoma, and Texas. Furthermore, RAM provides disaster relief in other countries like Haiti and Nepal as well as in the states. Care includes doctors, dentists, nurses, optometrists and veterinarians to do everything from eye-care to cancer screenings. To do this, they use quality technologies designed in mobile fittings, and in 2015, delivered medicine by drone for an event in Wise County, Virginia.[4]

Since his award winning in 2010, RAM has grown exponentially, and Brock, despite his eighty-two years, continues to work tirelessly, ensuring all projects and events run smoothly. He maintains a simple lifestyle, living out of his office, sleeping on the floor and subsisting on a diet of fruits, oatmeal, and water. He takes no income and devotes all of his time and energy to serving the people, whether by leading events or by reading the many emails patients send in. Brock's passion for service and equal healthcare is an example to all that we must not wait to make a change but rather help where we can.

Notes

1. R. F. Graboyes. "Care on the Margins—Stan Brock and RAM," Inside Sources, March 07, 2017, http://www.insidesources.com/care-margins-stan-brock-ram/.
2. "Meet Our Founder," April 10, 2018, https://www.ramusa.org/meet-our-founder/.
3. R. Blakely and K. Lay. "Dental Care Pioneer Stan Brock Wants to Bring Megaclinics to Britain," December 23, 2017, https://www.thetimes.co.uk/article/dental-care-pioneer-stan-brock-wants-to-bring-mega-clinics-to-britain-d7f9sd8kc.
4. A. Leve. "Saint Stan Brock: Who Are You?" n.d., http://www.ariel-leve.com/all-articles/sunday-times-magazine/features/saint-stan-brock-who-are-you/.

Beatrice Mtetwa, 2011 Inamori Ethics Prize Recipient
Roston Shore

Beatrice Mtetwa first received her LLB from the University of Botswana and Swaziland in 1981 and worked as a prosecuting attorney for the following two years. In 1983, Mtetwa decided to move to Zimbabwe, where she continued to work as a prosecutor until 1989. During this work, Mtetwa became increasingly concerned about the selectivity of the prosecutions she was observing. In 1989, Mtetwa moved to private practice, and soon thereafter, she began her highly influential work pertaining to human rights law in 1990.[1]

Fueled by a virtuous passion to protect and help people in need, wrongly treated and prosecuted, Mtetwa began her efforts to fight injustice in Zimbabwe. Her work for human rights preservation, especially the rights and treatment of journalists both native to Zimbabwe and those foreign, earned Mtetwa the International Press Freedom Award in 2005. The actions that earned her this award also put her at great personal risk as she threw herself into the frontlines to protect those who needed protection. She was additionally awarded the Burton Benjamin Memorial Award in 2008, making her the first person to ever be honored with both.[2]

Moving one more year forward, in 2009, Mtetwa was featured in a *New York Times* article for her part in freeing a reporter who had been wrongly arrested and placed into jail in Zimbabwe. Also in 2009, Mtetwa was awarded the Ludovic-Trarieux International Human Rights Prize, reserved each year to a lawyer who has exemplified the global defense of human rights, by activity or suffering, throughout his or her career. She was the second African—the other being Nelson Mandela—to ever receive this honor. 2010 brought Mtetwa the International Human Rights Award from the American Bar Association for her many efforts and successes in the realm of human rights law. Mtetwa is also a founding member and on the board of Zimbabwe Lawyers for Human Rights and was the past president of the Law Society of Zimbabwe.[3]

All these efforts and righteous acts of Mtetwa's led her to be awarded the 2011 Inamori Ethics Prize, presented by the Inamori International Center for Ethics and Excellence. Mtetwa's constant work and placing herself in the middle of conflicts to help those in need was more than enough to secure her place among the other winners of this prize. Since the Inamori Ethics Prize, Mtetwa has continued her fight for the rights of people wrongfully accused and prosecuted.

In 2013, Mtetwa herself fell victim to the types of wrongful prosecution she fights so earnestly to prevent. Mtetwa was at a house when police suddenly arrived and began to forcefully raid it. During their raid, Mtetwa asked for a warrant that would give them permission to search the house upon arrival. The police detained her and claimed that she was shouting at the top of her lungs that their actions were "unconstitutional, illegal, and unlawful." This case was taken to court, where the court ruled that none of the accusations were warranted or held up enough to continue processes. Rather than discouraging her from future endeavors and efforts, however, this case gave even more fuel to Mtetwa's righteous fire for human rights.[4]

In 2014, Mtetwa was awarded the International Women of Courage Award for more than twenty years of fighting against global injustice, defending press freedom, and upholding strong rules of law. She often accepted very difficult cases that other lawyers would not want to take on, out of fear of political reprisal. Mtetwa additionally defended two previous Women of Courage Award recipients, Jestina Mukoko and Jenni Williams.[5]

Mtetwa received an Honorary Doctorate from the University of Law at their graduation ceremony in December of 2015, along with Dame Janet Smith. The University of Law also published an article in which Mtetwa shares much of her story, and some of the specific detail as to why she chose to pursue human rights as fiercely as she does, and why the opposition and force used by her opponents do not scare her away from fighting for human rights.[6]

Most recently, Mtetwa fought to secure release letters of leaders of the Zimbabwe National Liberation War Veterans Association, taken into custody at the time by the Mugabe regime. This is not unique in the regard that over the past few years, Mtetwa has fought with the Mugabe regime over other critical human rights cases that the regime has brought into being through wrongful and right-infringing persecutions. Mtetwa continues her efforts daily and refuses to back down at the sight of forceful opposition.[7]

Notes

1. "Mtetwa Wins 2010 International Human Rights Award," *American Bar Association*, https://apps.americanbar.org/litigation/committees/international/ihr_2010.html.
2. "Beatrice Mtetwa," *Front Line Defenders*, Feb. 15, 2016, www.frontlinedefenders.org/en/profile/beatrice-mtetwa.
3. "Beatrice Mtetwa," *Front Line Defenders*.
4. "Beatrice Mtetwa," *Front Line Defenders*.
5. "Beatrice Mtetwa," *Front Line Defenders*.
6. "Profile: Beatrice Mtetwa, Recipient of U Law Honorary Doctorate 2015," *The University of Law*, Dec. 4, 2015, www.law.ac.uk/blog/profile-beatrice-mtetwa/.
7. "#IndexAwards2006: Beatrice Mtetwa, Campaigning," *Index on Censorship*, May 4, 2017, www.indexoncensorship.org/2017/04/indexawards2006-beatrice-mtetwa-campaigning/.

David Suzuki, 2012 Inamori Ethics Prize Recipient
Jacob Sandstrom

David Suzuki, the prominent Canadian geneticist and environmentalist, received the Inamori Ethics Prize at Case Western Reserve University in 2012. A resident of Vancouver, British Columbia, Suzuki is an advocate for science, the environment, and humankind in Canada and abroad. Throughout his life, David Suzuki has long worked to preserve and protect the planet through education and research. As an internationally recognized public figure in environmental activism, Suzuki encourages thoughtful approaches to dealing with environmental and scientific woes to ensure sustainability for generations to come.

Suzuki's academic work is thoroughly impressive, yet his ability to explain scientific complexities in "a compelling, easily understood way" has been the source of his acclaim worldwide.[1] An enthusiasm for science combined with a knack for speaking in a straightforward, accessible manner has afforded Suzuki the opportunity to educate millions on the importance of the natural world. The host of *The Nature of Things*, a CBC-TV program in its fifty-eighth season, Suzuki fascinates viewers with "adventure, drama and insight" by exposing the "wonder and accomplishments of science."[2]

The success of *The Nature of Things* has led to Suzuki's appearance in recent years on multiple channels, documentaries, and programs, including PBS, BBC, CBC Radio, and Discovery Channel, among others.[3] The program maintains a large viewership, providing a high-profile platform to share and celebrate scientific achievements while also drawing attention to areas in need of further attention, research, and action. Suzuki's continuing efforts as a broadcaster are impressive and make a tangible impact within and beyond the scientific community.

Apart from his weekly appearances on television, Suzuki is a prolific writer, having written more than fifty books, many of which are for children.[4] In 2015, David Suzuki published *Letters to My Grandchildren*, a collection of letters chronicling his own life and legacy, challenging his grandchildren—and readers worldwide—to "speak out and act on their beliefs" and to "live with courage, conviction, and passion."[5] Suzuki recognizes that meaningful change comes with time, effort, and resolve; he often implores future generations to continue the meaningful work that has defined his life.

In addition to his books, David Suzuki regularly writes articles and opinion pieces for news sources around globe. Writing in *The Guardian*, Suzuki notes that "climate change isn't a problem of the future. It's happening now. We're seeing the increasing effects of climate change every day."[6] He further calls humankind to action, adding that it is key to "move forward with a common understanding that we are embedded in the natural world, and what we do to our surroundings, we do to ourselves."

David Suzuki has received myriad awards, honorary degrees, and recognitions throughout his life for his tireless efforts to conserve the natural world. Since receiving the Inamori Ethics Prize, he has been recognized by numerous organizations, and was awarded Freedom of the City in 2015, the highest award given by the City of Vancouver on the basis of national or international achievement.[7] Suzuki's work has not only influenced his city and country, but also millions of global citizens today and tomorrow.

The David Suzuki Foundation, founded in 1990 and based in Vancouver, serves as a catalyst for sustainability and conservation, furthering the vision of David Suzuki. The continuing work of Suzuki and his Foundation is vast, including areas relating to sustainable transportation, tribal protected areas, eco-assets, safe drinking water, fisheries, coastal waters, and many others.[8] Ultimately, Suzuki believes that there is certainly hope for the future, but that hope comes with the caveat that we remember that "our dominance on Earth comes with great responsibility."[9]

Notes

1. "The Nature of Things: Host: David Suzuki," CBC-TV, April 19, 2018. http://www.cbc.ca/natureofthings/host/.
2. "The Nature of Things: About the Show," CBC-TV, April 19, 2018. http://www.cbc.ca/natureofthings/about/.
3. "The Nature of Things: Host: David Suzuki."
4. "About: David Suzuki," David Suzuki Foundation, April 19, 2018. https://davidsuzuki.org/expert/david-suzuki/.
5. "Letters to My Grandchildren," Greystone Books, April 19, 2018. https://greystonebooks.com/products/letters-to-my-grandchildren.
6. David Suzuki, "Rivers Vanishing into Thin Air: This Is What the Climate Crisis Looks like," *The Guardian*. April 21, 2017. Accessed April 19, 2018. https://www.theguardian.com/commentisfree/2017/apr/21/rivers vanishing-thin-air-climate-crisis.
7. "Freedom of the City," City of Vancouver, January 26, 2015. Accessed April 19, 2018. http://vancouver.ca/your-government/freedom-of-the-city.aspx.
8. "Projects," David Suzuki Foundation. Accessed April 19, 2018, https://davidsuzuki.org/projects/.
9. David Suzuki, "The 'Age of the Human' May Not Become the Age of Destruction," *The Guardian*. December 17, 2015, April 19, 2018. https://www.theguardian.com/commentisfree/2015/dec/17/paris-climate-deal-cop21-age-of-the-human-destruction.

Yvon Chouinard, 2013 Inamori Ethics Prize Recipient
J. Lucas Hii

Since receiving the Inamori Prize in 2013, Patagonia CEO Yvon Chouinard has continued the vision that environmental responsibility can be coupled with a successful business. Recently, after the federal decision to reduce the size of two national monuments drastically, Patagonia published on their website an opposition to the action titled "The President Stole Your Land" and are now fighting to keep the land protected under the Antiquities Act. Bears Ears and Grand Staircase-Escalante National Monuments are prized natural areas in Utah that are appreciated by climbers, nature lovers, and the local Native American community alike.[1] Chouinard recently has increasingly vocalized opposition to federal directives to back out of climate agreements and a disregard for the decisions that would damage the environment.

Surprisingly branching out of gear and clothing sales, Patagonia started sponsoring regenerative organic agriculture. "Patagonia Provisions" brings the eco-friendly mentality to address a growing food crisis driven by the food industry's current model of mass production. Patagonia Provisions supports local food producers, and attempts to repair the food chain currently reliant on GMOs, pesticides and herbicides to maximize production and minimize cost.[2] Patagonia also has a worn wear initiative supporting the purchase and recycling of past clothing and gear, which reduces the carbon footprint and the ecological impact that the clothing industry has on the environment.[3] Patagonia Action Works also supports local grassroots activist organizations connecting people to address the environmental crisis.[4] On top of internally sponsored directives, Patagonia, under the initiative of Chouinard, is still part of the "1% for the Planet" network of businesses and nonprofits that work together to give back to the environment.[5]

A glance across the Patagonia website resembles a bulletin board more focused on social and environmental justice than selling clothing. A trip to the company blog "The Cleanest Line " will reveal myriad blog posts echoing the stories of the company's adventurous CEO, with a feature by Chouinard titled "Telling the Dam Truth."[6] The article addresses the misconception that the vast growth of green energy coming from dams is actually destructive and damaging to river ecosystems. As the reluctant CEO, Chouinard's life philosophy is best encapsulated in his own words:

"I never wanted to be a businessman, but now that I am, I am determined to use my company and my voice to help solve the world's great environmental challenges. At Patagonia, we've spent more than forty years trying to protect the wild places our customers and employees love, and encouraging others to join the fight to save our planet—including from threats that often go overlooked or are misunderstood."[7]

Outside of the business that was built from the back of a butcher shop in Ventura, CA, Chouinard is respected as a climber, kayaker, surfer, fisherman, and explorer of the wild parts of this beautiful planet.[8] This deep appreciation of nature can be observed in the core values that Patagonia and Chouinard display. A renowned climber with first ascents on iconic walls such as *El Capitan* and the *Dawn Wall,* Chouinard is a key pioneer of the growing sport of rock climbing including a more natural method of climbing rock: using cams, nuts, and carabineers that leave rock undamaged without the need to hammer in bolts.[9] On top of rock climbing, Chouinard has had multiple practical publications including *Climbing Ice, The Responsible Company: What We've Learned from Patagonia's First 40 years,* and the central philosophy of Patagonia contained in *Let My People Go Surfing.*

The sentiments expressed in Chouinard's philosophical manual for growing an environmentally responsible, respected company titled *Let My People Go Surfing* still ring true in the actions of the company as a whole, and the individual initiatives Chouinard supports.

Notes

1. "*The President Stole Your Land,*" Patagonia, 2017, http://www.patagonia.com/protect
-public-lands.html.
2. Yvon Chouinard, "*Patagonia Provisions: Why Food?,*" 2018, https://www
.patagoniaprovisions.com/pages/why-food-essay.
3. "*Worn Wear,*" Patagonia, 2018, https://wornwear.patagonia.com/.
4. "*Action Works,*" Patagonia, 2018, https://www.patagonia.com/actionworks/.
5. "*Why We Exist,*" 1% For the Planet, 2018, https://www.onepercentfortheplanet.org/
why-we-exist.
6. Yvon Chouinard. "*Telling the Dam Truth,*" 2018, https://www.patagonia.com/
blog/2018/04/telling-the-dam-truth/.
7. Yvon Chouinard. "*Telling the Dam Truth.*"
8. Yvon Chouinard and N. Klein, 1970. *Let My People Go Surfing: The Education of a
Reluctant Businessman, Including 10 More Years of Business Unusual* (Second ed.). New York:
Penguin Books.
9. Yvon Chouinard and N. Klein, *Let My People Go Surfing.*

Denis Mukwege, 2014 Inamori Ethics Prize Recipient
Ellen Kendall

Working as a physician at the Panzi Hospital in Bukavu, Democratic Republic of Congo (DRC), Denis Mukwege is known by the locals as "the man who mends women."[1] After his medical training at the Lemera Hospital, Mukwege was called to action seeing the insufficient medical care provided to female patients. In 1999, Mukwege founded the Panzi Hospital as a clinic for gynecological and obstetric care. Mukwege hoped to address maternal health issues in his clinic, but due to the violence against women during the armed conflict in the DRC, the Panzi Hospital has emerged as the treatment facility for the survivors of sexual violence.[2]

The armed conflict in the DRC began in 1995, and sexual violence has been used as a weapon of war against the women of the community since the beginning. Mukwege's first patient was a female who had been violently raped by men in uniform, and while he thought this case would be an exception, it has become his life's work.[3] Over time, the Panzi Hospital has treated over fifty thousand victims of sexual violence using their five-pillar holistic healing model. This model includes physical care, psychological support, community reintegration services, legal assistance, and education and advocacy.[4]

In an interview, Mukwege detailed a case where he operated on a young mother, then fifteen years later, on the daughter, and three years after that, on the granddaughter. After this case he was quoted saying, "by the time I was sewing up the second generation, I said to myself: 'the answers won't come from the operating theater.'"[5] Mukwege remains an active surgeon on staff at the Panzi Hospital, but he splits his time between the hospital and advocating for women's rights around the world. In 2012, Mukwege spoke at the United Nations, where he denounced the armed conflict in the DRC and sought justice for those who had violated the women of the community. Shortly after the speech at the UN, Mukwege was violently attacked, and his family was held at gunpoint at his home in the DRC. After a brief recovery period in Europe, Mukwege returned to the Panzi Hospital to work with his patients in spite of ongoing safety threats.[6]

In a landmark ruling in December 2017, eleven Congolese militia members were convicted of crimes against humanity for the rape of thirty-seven young children, ages eighteen months to eleven years old. This trial was historic for the victims of Kavumu, the organizations like the Panzi Hospital that have been supporting these rape victims, and the greater community of the DRC, who are seeing justice served to those who committed sexual violence. This trial was the first time that a sitting government official in the Congo was found guilty for crimes that he and his militia committed, and the defendants could not have been proven guilty without the medical evidence collected by Mukwege and his team while they treated these young victims at the Panzi Hospital.[7]

Mukwege has brought hope to the women of the DRC and awareness to the global community. He has dedicated his life to serving his community, to healing the women, and to advocating for change at an international level. He serves on the advisory committee for the International Campaign to Stop Rape and Gender Violence in Conflict,[8] is one of the founders of the International Centre for Advanced Research and Training (ICART),[9] and is a research collaborator of the Female Empowerment in Eastern DRC Project.[10] For his fearless pursuit of justice for the women of the DRC, Denis Mukwege has been awarded many honors in addition to the Inamori Ethics Prize (2014), such as the UN Human Rights Prize (2008), the Sakharov Prize for Freedom of Thought (2014) from the European Parliament, the Top Fifty World's Greatest Leaders (2016) from *Fortune Magazine*, and the Seoul Peace Prize Laureate (2016). He has been the subject of at least one major documentary film, *The Man Who Mends Women: The Story of Dr. Denis Mukwege*, and has reportedly been nominated multiple times for the Nobel Peace Prize.

Mukwege is leading the charge to end sexual violence in wars, and he is showing the rest of the world that justice will be served.[11]

Notes

1. Jackson Sinnenberg, "A Doctor Who Treats Rape Survivors Seen As Nobel Peace Prize Contender." NPR, Oct. 6, 2016, www.npr.org/sections/goatsandsoda/ 2016/10/06/496893413/doctor-who-helps-rape-survivors-is-shortlisted-for-nobel-peace -prize.
2. "About Dr. Denis Mukwege–Dr. Denis Mukwege Foundation." *Dr. Denis Mukwege Foundation*, www.mukwegefoundation.org/about-us/about-dr-denis-mukwege/.
3. Aryn Baker, "Platon: Portraits of Sexual Assault Survivors in Congo." *Time*, time.com/ platon-congo-denis-mukwege/.
4. "The Panzi Model." *Panzi Foundation*, www.panzifoundation.org/the-panzi-model-1/.
5. Eliza Anyangwe, "Rape in DR Congo: An Economic War on Women's Bodies." *CNN*, Cable News Network, Jan. 19, 2018, www.cnn.com/2017/10/19/africa/denis-mukwege -congo-doctor-rape/index.html.
6. "About Dr. Denis Mukwege." *Dr. Denis Mukwege Foundation*.

7. "Justice Is Delivered for the Children of Kavumu." *TRIAL International*, TRIAL International, Dec. 13, 2017, trialinternational.org/latest-post/justice-is-delivered-for-the
-children-of-kavumu/.
8. "Physicians for Human Rights." *Physicians for Human Rights–International Campaign to Stop Rape & Gender Violence in Conflict*, physiciansforhumanrights.org/issues/rape
-in-war/stop-rape-in-conflict.html.
9. "About." *ICART*, International Center for Advanced Research and Training, icart-bukavu.org/about/.
10. Ragnhild Nordås, "Female Empowerment in Eastern DRC." *PRIO*, Peace Research Institute Oslo, Jan. 2014, www.prio.org/Projects/Project/? x=1094.
11. "Dr. Denis Mukwege." *Panzi Foundation*, www.panzifoundation.org/dr-denis
-mukwege/.

Martha C. Nussbaum, 2015 Inamori Ethics Prize Recipient
J. Lucas Hii

Martha C. Nussbaum, the Inamori Prize winner in 2015, remains at the University of Chicago as the Ernst Freund Distinguished Service Professor of Law and Ethics. Also appointed in the Law School and Philosophy Department, she is an associate in the Classics Department, the Divinity School, and the Political Science Department. Nussbaum is also a member of the Committee on Southern Asian Studies, and a board member of the Human Rights Program. A recipient of fifty-six honorary degrees from universities and colleges both within the U.S. and internationally, Nussbaum is also a fellow of the British Academy, and a member of the American Academy of Arts and Sciences, as well as the American Philosophical Society.[1] Nussbaum most recently received both the American Philosophical Association's Philip Quinn Prize (2015) "in recognition of service to philosophy and philosophers, " and the Kyoto Prize in Arts and Philosophy (2016) for lifetime achievement in arts and philosophy.[2] The Kyoto Prize is awarded annually to honor those who have "contributed significantly to the scientific, cultural, and spiritual betterment of mankind" in each of three categories: Scientific Advancement, Basic Sciences, and Arts and Philosophy. Nussbaum has contributed tremendously to the philosophical tradition and as described by the Inamori Foundation has "introduced the notion of incorporating human capabilities (what each person is able to do or be) into the criteria for social justice, beyond the conventional theory of equality based on a social contract among rational individuals. She established a new theory of justice that ensures the inclusion of the weak and marginalized, who are deprived of opportunities to develop their capabilities in society, and has proposed ways to apply this theory in the real world."[3]

Since receiving the award in 2015, Nussbaum has released *Anger and Forgiveness: Resentment, Generosity, and Judgement*, in which the messy emotions of anger and forgiveness are explored in a neo-stoic view to push beyond our current conception, ultimately to flourish more fully. Her argument focuses mainly on the irrational nature of common anger, in which people seek conventional retribution via "payback." The other response to anger, Nussbaum argues, circulates in the realm of status, relying on narcissistic power and domination. Responses to anger may be well served to be replaced by forward looking compassion.[4] In the difficult arena of conceptualizing very human emotions, Nussbaum's work serves well to decipher the messy areas of human moral life.

More recently, Nussbaum co-authored a book with Saul Levmore as a collection of paired essays titled *Aging Thoughtfully: Conversations about Retirement, Romance, Wrinkles and Regret*. A response to the questions, concerns, and considerations that many face while aging, this conversation can provide valuable insight into how we may conceive aging differently. The book confronts many topics rooted in ageism including retirement, family, plastic surgery, and stigma surrounding the process. Focused on a specific time of life, the ideas, message and structure of these paired essays or responses serves well for any reader to consider the more troublesome aspects of life.[5]

Nussbaum's work has contributed significantly to the progress of modern philosophical tradition and continues to be crucial for an everyday conception of a good life. Best expressed in Nussbaum's own words:

> To be a good human being is to have a kind of openness to the world, an ability to trust uncertain things beyond your own control, that can lead you to be shattered in very extreme circumstances for which you were not to blame. That says something very important about the condition of the ethical life: that it is based on a trust in the uncertain and on a willingness to be exposed; it's based on being more like a plant than like a jewel, something rather fragile, but whose very particular beauty is inseparable from that fragility.[6]

Notes

1. *"Martha Nussbaum,"* The University of Chicago, 2018, https://www.law.uchicago.edu/faculty/Nussbaum.

2. *"Philip L. Quinn Prize,"* American Philosophical Association, 2018, http://www.apaonline.org/page/quinn.

3. *"Announcement of the 2016 Kyoto Prize Laureates,"* Inamori Foundation *Press Release*, 2016, http://www.inamori-f.or.jp/img/media/pdf_kyoto/Press_Release_e2016.pdf.

4. M.C. Nussbaum, *Anger and forgiveness: Resentment, generosity, justice* (New York: Oxford University Press, 2016).

5. M.C. Nussbaum and S. Levmore, *Aging Thoughtfully: Conversations About Retirement, Romance, Wrinkles, and Regret* (New York: Oxford University Press, 2017).

6. M.C. Nussbaum and B. Moyer, *"A World of Ideas–Martha Nussbaum,"* PBS, 1988.

Peter Eigen, 2016 Inamori Ethics Prize Recipient
Roston Shore

No stranger to the worlds of economic development and governance, Peter Eigen has worked in these fields for several decades. Eigen has also focused on and led movements dedicated to improved governance on the global scale and promoting efforts against corruption. His strong leadership has been apparent since the age of thirteen, when he led a group of friends on wild adventures. At seventeen, he founded a jazz club that flourishes to this day. And at nineteen, he formed a horse riding club which allowed a farmer to start a new business and led Eigen to become the head of the National Riding Association at twenty-three.[1]

Eigen is a lawyer by training, but has worked as a manager of programs for World Bank in Africa and Latin America. While working with World Bank, Eigen provided legal and technical assistance to the governments of Botswana and Namibia to strengthen their legal networks for mining investments.[2]

In 1993, Eigen founded the nongovernmental organization, Transparency International. Transparency International, as its name suggests, promotes transparency and accountability in international development. Eigen has also served as a member of Kofi Annan's Africa Progress Panel, and as a member of the board of multiple NGOs including Kabissa, focused on building the capacity of African nonprofits, and German Doctors. Additionally, he has served as a member of the Advisory Council of the Arnold-Bergstrasser-Institute in Freiburg.[3]

It was for these reasons that Eigen was awarded the Inamori Ethics Prize in September of 2016 from the Inamori International Center for Ethics and Excellence. At the time of the award ceremony, Transparency International held chapters in more than 110 nations. Transparency International continues to thrive as the global leading nongovernmental organization promoting transparency and accountability in development worldwide, while also exposing and fighting corruption in all forms.[4]

Since receiving his award in 2016, Peter Eigen has continued his battle against corruption and for transparency, both with Transparency International and with other nongovernmental organizations. Still very active in African governance and anti-corruption efforts there, Eigen addressed the first Regional Roundtable on Infrastructure Governance in Cape Town,

South Africa, during early November of 2017. At the time of this round-table, South Africa still had a fair amount of corruption present, but had still come a long way from where it had started, thanks to organizations like Transparency International. Eigen addressed the vital importance of transparency and openness for successful and sustainable infrastructure projects, and although South Africa as a nation has come quite a long way since anti-corruption efforts started, the fight is never over and there is always room for further improvement.[5]

Additionally, on April 23, 2018, Peter Eigen will be featured as the internationally-acclaimed keynote speaker for the Corporation for Economic Development of Curaçao, Korpodeko. Korpodeko is having its celebration of thirty-three years of a tripartite commitment to the contribution to a sustainable economy for Curaçao. On more than one instance in the past thirty-three years, Curaçao's economy has gone through some major changes. This celebration also brings to light the great need for transparency in the highest areas of influence in Curaçao's community. There is also a current government initiative to institute an "Integrity Chamber," which can act as a center for accountability and support for the community, yet another reason why Peter Eigen was selected as the perfect person to be the keynote speaker.[6]

Notes

1. "#LeadYoung—Peter Eigen: Fearless since 13, He's Changed the World's Mindset about Corruption." *Ashoka | Everyone a Changemaker*, Sept. 8, 2017, https://www.ashoka.org/en/story/leadyoung-peter-eigen-fearless-13-he's-changed-world%E2%80%99s-mindset-about-corruption.
2. "Short Bio," Transparency International, https://www.transparency.org/files/content/ourorganisation/ShortBio_PeterEigen_EN.pdf
3. "Short Bio," Transparency International.
4. "Inamori Center to Present Transparency International Founder Peter Eigen with Inamori Ethics Prize." *The Daily*, Sept. 6, 2016, thedaily.case.edu/inamori-center-to-present-transparency-international-founder-peter-eigen-with-inamori-ethics-prize/.
5. "Transparency Is Key to Corruption-Free Infrastructure." *CNBC Africa*, Dec. 12, 2017, www.cnbcafrica.com/apo/2017/12/11/transparency-is-key-to-corruptionfree-infrastructure/.
6. "33 Years Contribution Korpodeko." *Curaçao Chronicle*, Apr. 6, 2018, curacaochronicle.com/economy/33-years-contribution-korpodeko/.

Marian Wright Edelman, 2017 Inamori Ethics Prize Recipient
Vanitha Raguveer

Marian Wright Edelman was the 2017 Inamori Ethics Prize winner and stands as an exemplary model of ethical leadership and advocacy. As the founder and president of the Children's Defense Fund, she has served as a voice for underprivileged populations, working to ensure all children have the opportunity to succeed with a "Healthy Start, Head Start, Fair Start, Safe Start and Moral Start to life."[1]

The first black woman admitted to the Mississippi Bar, Edelman graduated from Yale Law School and went on to lead the NAACP Legal Defense and Educational Fund in Mississippi. She went on to work for the counsel for the Poor People's Campaign, then found the Washington Research Project, serve as the Director of the Center for Law and Education at Harvard University, and then start the Children's Defense Fund in 1973. Through the past almost fifty years, she has received over one hundred honorary degrees, the Albert Schweitzer Humanitarian Prize, the Heinz Award, the MacArthur Foundation Prize Fellowship, the Presidential Medal of Freedom, and the Robert F. Kennedy Lifetime Achievement Award for her many writings. These writings include but are not limited to: *The Sea Is So Wide and My Body is So Small: Charting a Course for the Next Generation*; *Lanterns: A Memoir of Mentors*; *Guide My Feet: Prayers and Meditations on Loving and Working for Children*; and so many more.[2]

In her time since the Inamori Awards Ceremony in September, Edelman has continued to act as a voice of reason and passion for civil rights in America. Almost immediately following the awards ceremony, she spoke at the Association for the Study of African American Life and History annual conference in Cincinnati, Ohio. She was also awarded an honorary Doctor of Humane Letters from Ohio State University in December. Over the last year, she has been an integral part in California's banning of "Lunch Shaming," or lunchroom practices that humiliate public school children for unpaid lunch debts. This bill went into effect on January 1, 2018, and combats one of the various ways, big and small, that inequality can subsist.[3]

On April 4, at the National Civil Rights Museum's event, *An Evening of Storytelling*, commemorating the fiftieth anniversary of the assassination of Martin Luther King Jr., she spoke at a panel discussion with other civil rights leaders including Rep. John Lewis (D-GA), Diana Nash, Gina Belafonte and

Tamika Mallory.[4] On April 6, she gave the keynote address at the Beloved Community Talks Symposium at the King Center in Memphis, Tennessee.[5]

Most recently, she was featured in an HBO documentary called *The King in the Wilderness*, doing interviews to help shed light on Martin Luther King Jr.'s last few years. The documentary aired in early April.[6] She was also featured in Deborah Santana's anthology, *All the Women in My Family Sing*, which features narratives by sixty-nine women of various ages in efforts to shed light on the culturally dynamic struggles of women.[7]

In the coming weeks, she will be speaking with Gloria Steinem, women's rights advocate, and Michel Martin, weekend host of NPR's *All Things Considered*, at the Peace and Justice Summit held at the Montgomery Performing Arts Center in Montgomery, Alabama, on April 26, to celebrate the opening of the National Memorial for Peace and Justice and the Legacy Museum: From Enslavement to Mass Incarceration.[8] On May 20, she will also be receiving an honorary doctorate from La Salle University at their commencement ceremony. She will also be featured in the new Netflix documentary *Bobby Kennedy for President*, premiering on April 27, 2018.

Marian Wright Edelman remains one of the strongest speakers against inequality in America, using her voice to inspire younger movements and reflect on the current political climate. From calling on Congress to act on the Deferred Action for Childhood Arrivals Program (DACA) and the Children's Health Insurance Program (CHIP) before the government shutdown, or encouraging students at the March for Our Lives, she reminds us that "we must move forward together to keep our children safe."[9]

Notes

1. "Marian Wright Edelman," April 18, 2018, http://www.childrensdefense.org/about/leadership/marian-wright-edelman/.
2. "Marian Wright Edelman—Living Legends," Library of Congress, April 2000, https://www.loc.gov/about/awards-and-honors/living-legends/marian-wright-edelman/.
3. D. Mansini, "Mansini and The Meatball Chronicles Brings an Italian Brand of 'Actorvism' to Los Angeles," March 15, 2018, http://www.prweb.com/releases/2018/03/prweb15320695.htm.
4. N. Shelton, "Martin Luther King Assassination 50th Anniversary," March 26, 2018, https://www.c-span.org/blog/?4152/martin-luther-king-assassination-50th-anniversary.
5. N. Staff, "King Center, Millennium Gate Museum to Honor King on Death Anniversary," March 31, 2018, http://www.mdjonline.com/neighbor_newspapers/northside _sandy_springs/community/king-center-millennium-gate-museum-to-honor-king-on-death/article_bb7b36e4–34f3–11e8-bfae-8f8c31160ac4.html.
6. H. Stuever, "Review: HBO Documentary About MLK's Final Years Shows an Exhausted, Conflicted Hero," April 1, 2018, https://www.washingtonpost.com/entertainment/tv/hbo-documentary-about-mlks-final-years-shows-an-exhausted-conflicted-hero/2018/04/01/dcb5cffe-339f-11e8-8abc-22a366b72f2d_story.html?.

7. M. Rhor. "Anthology by Deborah Santana Celebrates Strength, Resilience of Women of Color," March 28, 2018, https://www.chron.com/life/article/Anthology-by-Deborah-Santana-celebrates-strength-12784554.php.

8. "The Roots, Common and Full Schedule for Peace and Justice Opening Week," April 19, 2018, https://www.birminghamtimes.com/2018/04/the-roots-common-and-full-schedule-for-peace-and-justice-opening-week/.

9. M. W. Edelman "Let's Move Forward Together," April 1, 2018, https://www.charlestonchronicle.net/2018/04/01/lets-move-forward-together/; M. W. Edelman "Action: Congress Must Do the Right Thing on: CHIP, DACA, and OPIODS Crises," January 27, 2018, http://www.blackstarnews.com/us-politics/justice/action-congress-must-do-the-right-thing-on-chip-daca-and-opiods.

Strategic Dissent
Obedience, Choice, and Agency for the Military Officer

Reuben Brigety
Dean of the Elliott School of International Affairs of
The George Washington University

Ladies and Gentlemen, good morning. Shannon, George, Marty, other friends, colleagues, it's my great honor to be with you here in the balmy climate of Cleveland, to help start off this amazing conference. Let me also again congratulate you, Shannon, and the Inamori Center for all the work you've done here over the years and for this amazing new facility that you have.

What I'd like to do with my remarks, which I hope we can follow with a robust conversation to get us going, is think through the question of strategic dissent for the military officer and also by extension by others, civilians that may also be involved in the defense and national security enterprise. It has been some time since I've been an active scholar of military ethics. However, in the time that I've been away from scholarship, I've been busy and have lived these issues both as a practitioner in the field in working on not only a series of refugee and policy related issues in Africa, but also a series of working closely with my military colleagues on a series of direct action military matters as well. I bring that sensibility as well to the work that we do at the Elliott School, which I'll talk about at the end of my talk.

I say all that to say that while I have been away from the subject as an active scholar, I continue to be interested, at times even obsessed, with the question of dissent—its role in not only the shaping and conduct of policy, but also its role in a very personal matter, a very personal way for the individual that is often charged with executing, or standing by, or watching some of the most weighty events, not only of national security, but frankly of import for individual human lives. One of the reasons that I find the question of dissent of particular importance in the military context is that, of course, at first look it seemed to be antithetical to the entire military enterprise. Lisa Layman might suggest that that might be the case.

Why might that be the case? Because, again, from not only from the outside, but also from a series of strictures how military life is governed. Obedience and discipline are at the core of the military profession, and not

not simply arbitrarily, but because, of course, discipline, which implies obedience to orders, certainly obedience to legal orders, is necessary in order to break through or control the so-called fog of war and the sorts of chaos that happens in the battlefield. That, therefore, is necessary in order to achieve victory on the battlefield or at sea. That is also necessary in order, as Auschwitz aficionados would recognize, to achieve the political objectives for which one uses force in the first place. If one follows that train of logic, one can assume by the transit of property of ethics that obedience is tied to achieving the political ends for the use of force.

What happens, however, if that theory is wrong or if, on certain occasions, one can actually help achieve the political objectives for which one is actually engaging in the use of force, not by obeying, but by dissenting? There are any number of models, any number of circumstances, any number of real world examples by which one can suggest this actually might be the theory that we ought to be thinking about, at least in certain circumstances, whether it be the very well known, well-publicized examples of My Lai on the one hand and Abu Ghraib on the other. Or whether it be any number of drone strikes that may have led to civilian casualties in environments where one had hoped they were trying to actually cultivate the population to support our political objectives, even as one prosecutes conflict against known or suspected terrorist subjects. Or leave aside the question of these high stakes, high profile uses of force.

What if what we're talking about in certain circumstances is the ability to dissent against an officer or a superior that one knows is taking illegal or unethical action, whether it be accepting a dinner party, or access to prostitutes, or Lady Gaga tickets when a junior officer thinks that might not be the case? Or what if what we're talking about is not on that level of professional personal conduct, but rather broader questions of policy? What role is there for the officer who thinks, "You know, I'm not sure that the intelligence actually suggests that there's weapons of mass destruction in this particular location?" What is one supposed to do?

Of course this is important, not only from these sorts of real world examples, but also frankly from questions of ethical theory, because as those of you who obviously are far more esteemed in the area of professional ethics know, one of the most important questions of ethics is not only how do we know what is ethical, but also the question of agency. In essence, it is almost irrelevant, certainly merely academic if one is simply talking about what the right ethical decision is if the individual actor does not have the quality of agency to be able to make an informed decision and indeed be able to act on whatever the ethical analysis may be. Herein lies the fundamental rub for the military officer. On the one hand, she is trained to obey orders. She's also trained to assume that the chain of command by which she receives these orders is acting legally, acting ethically, and also acting in support of the national interest.

If that is the default position of the institution, then . . . there are several questions that result from that. The first is, how do you know that that series of assumptions is actually operative, which is to say that the orders that one receives are legal, are ethical, and are in the national interest? Second, let's assume that one can accept the legal analysis. What is the ethical framework by which one is even to interpret even what might essentially otherwise be legal orders? Is it one's own personal religious conviction? Is it what one understands to be the broader ethical frame of one's country? Is it something else, and how does one have access, and how does one be able to adjudicate those sorts of ethical choices?

The third really quite important question is that even if one can identify the right level of analysis, are we talking about battlefield decision? Are we talking about high policy? Are we talking about questions of individual conduct? Even if one can affirmatively understand the normative structures that are available to help adjudicate those questions, whether it be matters of law or ethics, then you get to one series of systemic issues. What systems are in place to be able to actively act on such dissent, or at least to be able to raise such questions? This is actually a crucially important point and it's crucially important if, for no other reason, that there are actually multiple different models that are available, not only in the military, but amongst different militaries and indeed amongst different professions.

Let me give you a couple of examples. As George mentioned, I spent six years in the State Department. One, the US State Department was modeled, the Foreign Service State Department was modeled on the US military, so, although they don't wear uniforms, there is obviously a question of hierarchy. There are ranks that are meant to be expected and it's also based on the general proposition that particularly when you're trying to implement and execute policy halfway around the world, there has to be some level of discipline between what is decided in capitols and what is actually executed on the ground, in that sense, not unlike sending a ship at sea.

Yet, because one's thinking about these questions of policy that can often be complicated, there is, as you may know, a formal dissent channel within the State Department, through which any diplomat can actually raise questions or concerns about the policy that he is actually meant to actually execute. Not only is there a formal channel for dissent, there is (at least there used to be prior to) in the previous administration, there traditionally has been a formal reward for the best dissent report in the State Department on any given year. Why is that important? Because it shows to the institution what respectful dissent ought to look like, and how it ought to be rewarded, and what the expectations are of the institution for how dissent can actually be valuable to the mission of the institution as a whole.

Let's take another example from medicine, which is another discipline where particularly in the context of surgery or triage, there is hierarchy from physicians, to nurses, to physician assistants, etc., where there is an expectation that a doctor's request for the patient will be followed. In fact, those requests are called orders in the medical environment, and also where there is the assumption that in the operating theater, the surgeon is the highest authority, not only as a matter of law, but because the surgeon has the most in technical experience about the procedure. As a result of a series of challenges with regard to medical mistakes in the United States over the last decade, what is now common practice serving in surgery rooms across the United States, is that everybody in the operating theater is now empowered, whether they are the surgeon, or a nurse, or a surgical tech to stop or raise their hand at any given time to say, "I see something that does not look right," even if they may not happen to be the most senior person in the room.

I raise this to say that, and there are other examples from aviation. There are other examples from oil drilling, particularly in light of the Deepwater Horizon fiasco and others. There are other examples in which one is actually from other disciplines, from other professions, in which one actually recognizes, not only that dissent is not inherently bad, but actually can be vital to achieving the appropriate mission of the institution, and they have enabled systems to be able to do that.

The final question that I have and the final area that I would posit for discussion, is that in addition to levels of analysis, in addition to questions of the moral framework to make decisions, in addition to questions of system, are questions of training and incentives. This is the most difficult part, I would argue, certainly in the military context. How does one simultaneously train a person to charge the hill, to take out the machine gun nest, and to obey the lawful order of those appointed over them and also train them to not only be comfortable with, but indeed the necessity of speaking up with dissent when they see that something is antithetical to the mission, values, law that govern the organization? I would submit to you that this is the greatest challenge that certainly in the context of multiple military environments that we face. It's a challenge for a variety of reasons.

One, even for the most wise, experienced amongst us, living with those two fundamental tensions in one's head, even in an academic environment, is incredibly challenging. It's even more challenging under the strains of real world operations, when you're really at sea or you're really engaged in combat, and the people against whom you must dissent are also the people on who you must depend for your own life. That's really hard, and yet, don't we all wish that more people had more of a desire to speak up earlier during Abu Ghraib? Don't we all wish that more people had the opportunity to speak up and challenge Lt. Calley earlier, so that My Lai would never have been a stain on the record of the United States in the first place? Don't we all wish that more Lt. Commanders, or Commanders, or Jr. Lieutenants had said something when they saw this contractor in the 7th Fleet doing all kinds of shady things, that have now fundamentally upset an entire generation of Naval officers and put into question frankly our entire position in all of East Asia from a Naval perspective?

I don't know what the answers to these four questions are on a practical basis. As I say, I have to run a school so I don't have as much time to actually sort of think about them myself, but I do know that these are the questions, at least these four, that must dominate our thinking in this area. Accordingly, one of the things—although I don't have time to write about it—one of the great things about being Dean is that you actually have an opportunity to set up programs. One of the things that we have done, two things we've done at the Elliott School (which George said correctly, is the largest school of international affairs in the United States—we have almost 3,200 students) is we have articulated a vision for what we're doing at the Elliott School— this is—that we characterize it as the acronym STEP, S-T-E-P, which stands for achieving elite excellence in scholarship, teaching, ethics, and practice.

The reason we have ethics in our core mission, as I tell all of our students, that international affair students are a special breed of student, because by definition they care about the state of the world and they want to prepare themselves to go off and fight the world's fight. "If you do so," I tell our students, "I can guarantee you, you will face very challenging ethical problems. Thus, it is vital for us, while you are here in our scholarly community, that we give you the best preparation to know what doing the right thing feels like, and that we also give you, not only the background knowledge, but help to sort of develop your courage to be able to do the right thing when your time of questioning comes."

Accordingly, the second thing we've done is we've established something that we're calling the LEAP Academy, which stands for the Leadership Ethics and Practice Academy, which amongst other things has, as its responsibility, teaching ethics across all of our curricula for our international affair students at the undergraduate and graduate level, creating a series of lecture series and other events to actually show our students what practical, ethical decision-making actually looks like, and the fact that you can actually make ethical decisions and survive. You can actually dissent without having to throw away your career. You can actually stand up and be counted and live to tell the story as opposed to the fears that if one stands up in a variety of different ways, that will be the very last thing that you can do.

We're doing so, as I say, because we think that not only is it important for us to do, but quite frankly we also hope that other similarly placed institutions will also place a similar importance on ethics in international affairs, because we don't see this as a competition. We actually sort of see this as part of the community. All of us are trying to do our very best to train the next generation of young people to go off and fight the world's fight.

Let me conclude my opening remarks before we go into what I hope will be an interesting question and answer session debated amongst ourselves, by reiterating something that George said, and that is that what all of you are doing as scholars and also as practitioners in this space of professional military ethics could not be more vital and could not be more timely. One only has to take a look not only at the series of headlines that are happening politically in all of our countries, but also take a look at the really quite serious security challenges that we're facing in multiple parts of the world, and note that in addition to having the technical expertise to solve them, we also need people that are rooted in questions of fundamentally human dignity and also rooted in what it takes, as Dr. Inamori says, what does it take to be a decent human being and to bring that sensibility to their work?

Thank you very much. I look forward to our questions and more importantly, I wish you all the best for this wonderful conference here in Cleveland. Thank you.

FRENCH: First taker.

BRIGETY: Yes, Dr....

AUDIENCE MALE 1: [inaudible]

BRIGETY: I'm sorry. Before you say it, I actually sort of...I've learned something. I now know that in order to be the Editor of the Journal of Professional Military Ethics, your last name needs to be Cook and you need to be either currently or have been employed in the United States Air Force Academy, so I guess I'm doubly out. But please, continue.

AUDIENCE MALE 1: Nice to see you.

BRIGETY: Yes, sir.

AUDIENCE MALE 1: Two quicks. In the U.S. military, starting with the work of Don Snider in the Army about 20 years ago, a lot of the questions were interested in the framework of the question, is military service a profession or are we merely obedient bureaucrats, as Snider would put it?

BRIGETY: Right.

AUDIENCE MALE 1: And a lot of the training that's going on through the organizations in the army to stress the importance of helping people think of themselves as professionals.

BRIGETY: Yes.

AUDIENCE MALE 1: But one of the implications of that is, if you're truly a professional, then there's an internal ethic of things that you will and you won't do.

BRIGETY: Yes.

AUDIENCE MALE 1: There are things you could ask your doctor to do for you that they would simply refuse on the grounds...

BRIGETY: That's correct.

AUDIENCE MALE 1: ...that I can't do that...

BRIGETY: That's correct.

AUDIENCE MALE 1: ...in a way that's consistent with my professional obligation.

BRIGETY: That's correct.

AUDIENCE MALE 1: But they're clearly, the professions that you listed, are more firmly on the professional side and less on the bureaucratic side...

BRIGETY: Yes.

AUDIENCE MALE 1: ...than military service. Any thoughts about how that balance will help us either clarify or muddy the waters?

BRIGETY: Yes.

AUDIENCE MALE 1: Then the second point, an area I've gotten really interested in the last few years, is when military people talk about ethics, they talk usually in Aristotelian terms, in terms of character and integrity, and the ideas that individuals have these characteristics, and if they have them, then they're reliable, and they would be good to go in kind of any environment. But the literature and moral psychology shows that in fact context affects people's behavior...

BRIGETY: Yes.

AUDIENCE MALE 1: ...to almost incredibly counterintuitive ways, and so when you look at something like, oh, Fat Leonard scandal in 7th Fleet, my prediction is what's going to turn out to be true there is we send a few bad people there, but we also had a really bad environment in 7th Fleet.

BRIGETY: Yes. Yes.

AUDIENCE MALE 1: That signaled the people that when you come out here, unless you really want to be the standout, as the newbie you want to fit in.

BRIGETY: Right.

AUDIENCE MALE 1: All military organizations are like that and so whatever the espoused ethic of the organization is, we all know individual units have different ethics based on those environmental factors. You experienced that, I'm sure, within the State Department...

BRIGETY: Yes.

AUDIENCE MALE 1: ...in different subcultures in State. Just those two points. Any reflection about that?

BRIGETY: Sure. I think those are both excellent questions. First on the issue of whether or not the military is a profession or a collection of organized bureaucrats and what the implications of that are, I fall firmly, hardly on the side that it is a profession and must be a profession. Now, I don't think that the fact that it is a profession necessarily, and I'll come back to why I think that in a moment, I don't think that the fact that it's a profession is necessarily in tension with the law or legal strictures, because all of the other professions that I talked about, for example medicine, right, or the law, the law, that is a profession, I mean, not only are their canons of professional ethics but they're also governed by various state and in some cases federal law, about what they can or can't do, which is part of the reason why you need a license to practice, part of the reason why you can be sued, etc., etc., etc.

The fact that, for example, there is, in the U.S. context and with its analogs elsewhere, the U.S. Uniform Code of Military Justice (UCMJ), which requires certain legal aspects, certainly in regards to obedience, and obedience to orders necessarily, doesn't necessarily mean that there cannot be as well an accompanying, perhaps sometimes even a superseding code of ethics that goes above and beyond what the law in any particular case requires. Let me give you what I think is sort of the nightmare example of this. I'm going to try to state this as apolitically as I can based on what I understand to be some of the discussion.

In light of the rising tensions between the United States and North Korea on the Korean peninsula, with many in the foreign policy community, particularly in that horrid bastion of elitist sort of people that get it wrong, the Council on Foreign Relations, there is serious, has been serious concern that we have been at the closest possibility of a real world nuclear exchange since the Cuban Missile Crisis. As a result of this, there have been a number of rumors, none of which I have seen corroborated, but, which I have seen reported multiple times in what I would consider to be credible news outlets and also very real discussion as of matters of law about who has the authority to actually launch American nuclear weapons and does the President of the United States have sole authority to be able to do that.

As those who, particularly that I see at least one submariner in the audience, we know that America's nuclear deterrent was built for maximum efficiency and response time and less to create multiple redundancies for reflection at the highest levels. There are redundancies at the tactical level, dual key, whatever, but certainly at the highest level, the national command authority, one can reasonably ask, for senior military officers or senior civilians that are closest to the President and are part of the NCA, is there a professional military ethic of dissent or disobedience that could reasonably be called for in an environment where it is unclear that the launch of a nuclear weapon, particularly given the politics around that, is in the best interest of the country?

Now, that is not simply my assertion. As we know, this has actually been really quite actively sort of debated. But there are any number of other sort of further examples further down the line. I would, for example, refer you to, you know, one of our scholar at the Elliott School is a scholar named Hugh Gusterson. Many of you may know his work. He wrote this book last year called *Drone*, which talks about some of the ethics of use of remote vehicles or whatnot, and then I think that presents a whole other series of questions, so I fall firmly on the question that it must be a profession, that the nature of profession actually helps psychologically the individual military member, and that frankly we would actually do better, not only to embrace it as a profession, but actually not only as medicine and law has done, but actually do an awful lot more to tease out what that means, in particular as it relates to matters of dissent and what those lines of ethical beyond simply obeying lawful orders, what are the lines of appropriate conduct.

Which then gets to the second question. I also firmly believe that in addition to whatever anyone's individual predilections may be, context matters greatly. I absolutely believe that. I also believe, frankly, that in most cases most people are capable of most things, given the right or wrong set of circumstances. Our institutions assume that, which is not only why we sort of focus so much on the rule of law, but also why we spend so much time on training ethics. It's why we go to houses of worship regularly, because it's not the assumption that, for example, I'm a Christian, I would never say, "Yeah, I went to Sunday School once back in 1987. I'm good. I got it. Thank you very much," right? I mean, you sort of continue to exercise that ethical framework a great deal at an individual level, but it's also why it's crucially important for individual leaders and also for institutions to create that enabling environment.

If I may, I know we're live streaming, so I'm going to be very careful about how I say this next piece. The Fat Leonard scandal has, as I mentioned, sucked up an entire generation, maybe even two generations of naval officers, two of which I happen to know. They were both in my company when I was a Midshipmen in the Naval Academy. One happened to be a classmate of mine. The other happened to be a First Class Midshipman at Senior. One of whom, would have been the last person in the world I ever would have expected to be sucked into this environment literally.

As a matter of record, I have no independent knowledge of what I'm about say, but what I suspect could have happened is that this person, because of what I knew about him and also what I knew about his past conduct, probably tried to do the right thing initially, and then as a result of the total environment, as a result of what was happening amongst his superiors and seniors, eventually as, because we know what Fat Leonard's MO was, you know it got brought in a little bit closer, a little bit closer, and a little bit closer, and then decides, "Well, am I really going to be the sucker who's going to try to be the Boy Scout when clearly everybody knows that this is how business is done out here?"

One of the things I wonder is, how did the system fail somebody like that? In addition to whatever his own clear personal feelings were, why do we have a...What was happening such that so many other people who otherwise had very distinguished careers, then went to all the appropriate accession sources. They had all the mandatory ethical training. They'd all took their kids to synagogue, or a temple, or whatever on Sundays or Fridays, whatever. How did so many people get this so wrong over such a long period of time? I have to think that part of it is that we somehow failed systemically to create strictures where junior people at sea in very challenging environments far away from the flagpole were sufficiently empowered to be able to challenge what is clearly wrong behavior. Had we been able to shift that and created better strictures, it would have saved everybody an awful lot of heartache.

I actually have a rule when I do teaching and that rule is I insist on gender parity in questions, so I go gentlemen, ladies, gentlemen, ladies, so I'm going to open the floor to ladies first, and then we'll go back to another gentlemen. You're promised you'll be next. Ladies, is there a question? Yes Ma'am?

AUDIENCE FEMALE 1: Hi. My name is Lisa.

BRIGETY: We need you to wait for the microphone.

AUDIENCE FEMALE 1: Hi. My name is Lisa. I'm a military ethics MA student here at Case Western. My question had to do with what you were talking about with training and having people able to be able to dissent.

BRIGETY: Yes.

AUDIENCE FEMALE 1: One of the things that I was looking at in research was the lack of ethical training for enlisted members. This is just kind of my opinion, but it looks like, from what I've seen, there's a little bit of a bias against just regular enlisted members, thinking maybe they can't handle it. It's too much for them in terms of scholarship. How would you kind of recommend tying those two things together...

BRIGETY:: Yeah.

AUDIENCE FEMALE 1: ...so that you have enlisted members who have an ethical framework to work with to be able to know when they can dissent and then also to be able to have this system in place for them to dissent in what's a respectful and a useful way?

BRIGETY: Right. That's a great question, because it begs questions of sociology, begs questions of ethics, begs questions of the law. Let me just try to address it a little bit. Again, I can't claim any authority, maybe not even familiarity with what happens in our military from sister countries, but in the US military, for example in the US Marine Core the oaths that are taken by officers and enlisted people are different. As you know, the oath for an officer, "I solemnly swear to support and defend the Constitution of the United States, yada, yada, yada, so help me God." For a...Sorry, you know I get into it. I meant every word of it. For an enlisted person the oath includes, "And I promise to obey the lawful orders of those appointed over me." That part of the oath does not exist in the officer oath. It's written into what we expect of them.

I think and this is where I think kind of, a sociological aspect comes in, because, of course traditionally over centuries the officer core was drawn from a more highly educated elite social class while the enlisted ranks across services were drawn from lower socioeconomic classes. While some of that still exists, certainly in the American context, not only do we have the most highly educated military we have ever had at both the enlisted and officer levels, we also are operating environments increasingly, whereas, you know General Chuck Krulak is famous for coining the phrase, "The strategic corporal," right? The notion that even an enlisted person who's standing at checkpoint, or guarding a prison, or manning a launch site, or anything else can be placed in the position where their choices can actually have strategic consequences. If that is the case, I completely agree with you that we ought to be thinking about the questions of dissent, not only for officers, but also for enlisted people, even understanding that still the nature of their oaths, and the scopes of their presumed responsibility in the normal course of their duties are different.

Now, one of the other things I think it's important to note, and certainly in the context of a series of unfortunate training accidents going back a decade-and-a-half, we now at least have the, in training environment bootcamps and A schools, and things of that nature, have the concept of a training timeout, right? You know, so I, Private Schmotz, feel like I'm about to have a heart attack when we're on this run. "Call a training timeout." It's technically possible, but you better be right. But again this goes back to all the other sorts of things that we talked about before, that even if the presumption is obedience, that it's also important to train on dissent, to train and practice it, so that members of the military and civilians who work with them as well know,

like increasingly we do in the State Department, what appropriate dissent looks like, what appropriate dissent feels like, and also how one can dissent as a way of actually protecting both the mission and the institution itself.
  Yes Sir?

AUDIENCE MALE 2: Well, I'm [inaudible] Fellow at the Stockdale Center at Naval Academy this year.

BRIGETY: Go Navy! Beat Army!

AUDIENCE MALE 2: Indeed.

BRIGETY: Next year.

AUDIENCE MALE 2: I wanted to address the three assumptions that you mentioned.

BRIGETY: Sure.

AUDIENCE MALE 2: In terms of the norm of obedience.

BRIGETY: Right.

AUDIENCE MALE 2: Those seem to be the grounds of what you consider to be appropriate dissent. The first being legality. The second being compliance with an ethical code. The third being that the order's in the national interest. While I understand the first two, and we've spoken to them a little bit, the third seems to be particularly problematic.

BRIGETY: Yes.

AUDIENCE MALE 2: One that's not shared by necessarily many scholars of civil-military relations or others. Peter Fever, for example, would speak of the civilian's right to be wrong. I guess my question is, in the national interest as judged by whom...

BRIGETY: Yes.

AUDIENCE MALE 2: Because indeed when a military starts to have the ability to independently assess what's in the national interest, there's certainly a very well-respected school of thoughts that suggest that that short circuit self-determination and meaningful democratic participation, and so how is it that you would address that? It also raises the question then of obedience, not purely in the practical mode that you discussed...

BRIGETY: Right.

AUDIENCE MALE 2: ...in terms of the necessity to execute policy...

BRIGETY: Right. Right.

AUDIENCE MALE 2: But also as a duty...

BRIGETY: Yes.

AUDIENCE MALE 2: ...in which it takes an ethical value.

BRIGETY: Yes.

AUDIENCE MALE 2: I was wondering if you could speak to those.

BRIGETY: It's a great, great question and a very hard one. Let me give you a couple of reasonable examples. On the one hand of the argument is, you know, what you've suggested is Peter Fever's approach, which obviously has a great deal of merit, which is, if we...and let's posit that we're talking in American context and those that are similarly situated. If we live in a democracy, the people's will must be respected and civilian control of the military means that the military has to obey the policy direction of the elected government of the day even if one can reasonably debate the merits of the position that the government has taken.

Let me kind of...two very real world examples that have caused me to reflect about, at least that'll show why that is problematic. We are in the year 2017 and we still have forces in the field that are actively engaged in combat all over the world in a context of an authorization of use in military force that was authorized in 2001 for a very specific threat against Al Qaeda in Afghanistan, and then, which was subsequently spread to Iraq. It has spread more, and more, and more, and gotten thinner, and thinner, and thinner as we've gone along to the point where there have been at least some military officers who have taken to a greater or lesser extent, asked the question, "Do we still even have legally the authority to continue to actually sort of wage war on an increasingly sort of reed thin, you know, authorization and what is my responsibility as somebody who has sworn to uphold and defend, not the government of the day, but the Constitution of the United States to continue to wage war in what might otherwise be a questionable environment?"

Now, and that applies to, not only to sort of like kind of big, kind of macro question whether or not we're going to deploy, but whether or not we have eyes on this particular target of this particular bad person in this particular country on these two dates and we have these assets that could launch these weapons in this environment—and oh, by the way, if we do, we think we're actually going to have, you know, these sets of civilian casualties, right? I mean, these are actually sort of real, sort of, you know, fair questions.

I'll give you another example, a very recent one. I've spent more and more of my time in the last decade now working on Africa. One of the interesting things that has happened in US engagement with Africa in the last decade is the creation of the US-Africa Command, which is now ten years old this year. One of the things that those officers and enlisted people do is a series of military engagements all across Africa to strengthen indigenous African militaries, build strategic partnerships, etc. As you may know, the President of the United States recently expressed his view about the entirety of the continent of Africa. It was not favorable.

If you are a major who has to go lead a training detachment in Senegal or Mali and amongst the things you're doing, you know, as the end of the exercise, you have a local reporter who stands up, puts a microphone in your face and says, "So, Major Schmotz, we understand your Commander in Chief said this about Africa. Do you agree with your Commander in Chief about his assertion about all of our military?" How are you supposed to adjudicate that particular, in addition to like the jujitsu of how do you think through, you know, media training that maybe you did or didn't get before you left Stuttgart, right? I mean, how are you supposed to actively continue to develop a partnership when the Commander in Chief has laid out, frankly a very sort of different view of who your strategic partners ought to be and why?

I can credibly make the case that while I understand the general argument that questions of what is in the best national security interests of the country ought to be beyond the purview of making ethical decisions, particularly when it relates to potential dissent. I can also see, from real world examples, why frankly they ought to be, precisely because one can foresee the environment. This is why we're having the whole conversation of dissent. One can foresee the situation in which the civilian masters or the civilian leadership who, in the analysis I laid out, are presumed to be operating in a legal and ethical way, aren't. Thus, one could also make therefore the argument that perhaps the most important ethical decision that somebody could do at some other point down the chain is at minimum, flag the dissent and perhaps even sort of act on it. That's why these are really hard questions. Ladies?

FRENCH: We have time for one more.

BRIGETY: One more. Yes Ma'am?

AUDIENCE FEMALE 2: Obedience is vital...

BRIGETY: I'm sorry, your name, please, and your [crosstalk]...

AUDIENCE FEMALE 2: Oh, I'm sorry. Nikki Coleman. I'm from the Royal Australian Air Force. Go Air Force! Beat Navy!

BRIGETY: Maybe that works down under, but we have a different way here.

AUDIENCE FEMALE 2: No, no. I've lived at Annapolis. I understand. Obedience is vital to military culture.

BRIGETY: Yes.

AUDIENCE FEMALE 2: It's a profession unique, and I use that very selectively, compared to any other professional organization or job in regards to obedience and having to obey orders. It's the only profession where you can go to jail for disobeying a legal order.

BRIGETY: Correct.

AUDIENCE FEMALE 2: It's vital to military culture. In Australia, we have value statements for the Army, Navy, Air Force, for all of the overarching defense. We also have one for the Defense Force Academy and we have value statements for various different brigades and so on. None of those mention obedience at all, so I don't know how that is internationally. I'd like to hear if your militaries have them internationally. It begs the question, we want dissent obviously, because we don't want another My Lai, or Fat Leonard, or Abu Ghraib. But are we ready to actually encourage dissent if we can't put obedience... If we can't even talk about obedience...

BRIGETY: Yes.

AUDIENCE FEMALE 2: How do we then authentically talk about dissent?

BRIGETY: Right. That's why you are scholars and that's what your job is to do. I don't mean that to be too flippant. As much as to say that, you know, sometimes it is not unique to the military. Organizations often sometimes have the most difficulty in transforming themselves and asking sort of really difficult questions. Sometimes it takes people that are actually sort of enabled and can take some, not only by their position, if they're a tenured professor or whatnot, but also by virtue of being close enough to the organization, but not of it, in it but not of it, to be able to ask these hard questions. What is clear to me is that the normal, traditional, centuries old framework of obedience being the stop, start, end of military life is no longer valuable completely unchallengeable in a current strategic environment. Thus, one has to grapple with these hard questions of what does appropriate dissent look like and how do we talk about it? I don't know what the right answer is, but I certainly do know that, that is the appropriate question. I look forward to seeing additional scholarships and debates in that regard.

BRIGETY: Thank you so much for having me. I wish to give you my best wishes for a great conference. Thank you.

FRENCH: We'd like to thank you again.

BRIGETY: Thank you so much. Thank you.

FRENCH: Got a little gift for you.

BRIGETY: Thank you.

FRENCH: Thank you for launching us so well with so many excellent questions and insights from your own life experience. We are very grateful. I also appreciate hearing about the exciting programs and efforts at the Elliott School and we definitely agree that it shouldn't be a competition. We want many such programs and many things blooming all over, so that we can get in the kind of position to challenge and ask the questions that need to be asked. As you just clarified, sometimes we are the only ones who can do that, so we have to take that role very seriously.

Bridging the Canyon
Coming to Terms with Cross-Cultural Differences in Ethical Leadership

Howard Ernst
Professor of Political Science, United States Naval Academy

Abstract

In the spring of 2017, the Stockdale Center for Ethical Leadership at the United States Naval Academy sponsored a training program for a small group of Naval Academy faculty and staff members. The first of its kind program involved a group of fourteen influential members of the Naval Academy community (including civilian professors, varsity coaches, and military leaders). The participants engaged in an intensive outdoor leadership program under the guidance of the National Outdoor Leadership School (NOLS), a well-established organization that teaches leadership through challenging outdoor experiences). The Naval Academy group traveled to the Canyonlands of Utah and spent a week overcoming physical obstacles and engaging in leadership exercises. The result was a clash of leadership styles that resulted in members of the group rethinking their assumptions regarding ethical leadership.

It was our first full day in the Canyonlands of southeastern Utah. It had been planned by our NOLS instructors as a relatively light day of hiking. We were to enter White Canyon between mile markers 81 and 82 off of Route 95 (between Hite Marina and the Natural Bridges National Monument), just below what is known as Atomic Rock. Our plan, which looked easy enough on paper, was a modest drop into the canyon followed by what our NOLS leaders estimated would be a four-hour hike along a marked path, past the beautiful Kachina Bridge and the stunning Native American ruins at Horse Collar Ruin, to our desired campsite just outside of the Natural Bridges Monument area in Deer Canyon.

Ten hours and several formidable obstacles later, we had finally staggered to our campsite in Deer Canyon, or so we thought. One reason that we had hiked longer and pushed ourselves harder than we had intended on day one was that no camping is allowed in the Natural Bridges Monument. So once we entered that area, we had little choice but to carry on, even if the path was longer and more difficult than our instructors had planned. You can imagine our relief when we dumped our packs and began to settle in and enjoy the last remaining sunlight of the day.

Our relief quickly turned to frustration when, with packs emptied, hiking shoes off, socks drying on rocks, and cooking teams activated, we were informed that someone had found a marker for the Natural Bridges National Monument posted on a large tree a few hundred yards up Deer Canyon from where we had emptied our packs. It appeared that we might have set up camp too early and we were still in the restricted area of the Natural Bridges National Monument. After carefully referencing the maps, we were confident that we were in fact out of the restricted area and concluded that the reason the sign was posted up canyon from us was that it was attached to the only large tree in the area, one of the few truly substantial trees we had seen all day. Nevertheless, the instructions were handed down by our NOLS leaders that we were to repack our bags and move a few hundred yards up-canyon, past the misplaced sign.

It was in this atmosphere of fatigue and frustration that I was to give my "leadership journey." Each day, three participants were appointed as designated Leaders of the Day. I was one of the three leaders on day one. At the end of the day, there is a period of reflection in which each leadership team provides positive feedback to their leader as well as constructive tips for improving their leadership approaches. Following the team feedback sessions, the fourteen members of the overall expedition meet for the culminating event of the day, in which that day's designated leaders give talks known as "leadership journeys."

The leadership journeys are intended as fairly short (eight- to ten-minute) testimonials in which the designated leaders explain some important event or milestones that impacted their journey toward becoming a leader. Most of the leadership journeys are grounded in personal experiences, but they also give insights into the individual's personal leadership philosophy and their personality. They are often remarkably personal reflections in which participants thoughtfully share private aspects of their lives. But after the long day of hiking, followed by the unpacking, repacking, and unpacking again, I had little time, energy or, frankly, interest in preparing my talk.

But even if I'd had more time and energy, it would have been a daunting task giving a leadership talk to this particular group. Our group consisted of distinguished naval officers, military professors in the Leadership Department of the Naval Academy, division one varsity coaches, and accomplished outdoor leadership instructors, as well as a few rag-tag civilian professors. I fall squarely into the last category. My daily leadership decisions typically revolve around deciding if I should work from home or venture onto campus, whether I should have tea or coffee in the morning, whether I should grade papers, update lectures, or give attention to research projects. The life of a college professor is mostly a solitary endeavor, and when decisions need to be made, they are typically low stakes affairs.

Rather than lecture my new friends on the finer points of leadership, I decided to be completely honest with the group. I explained to them my perspective on leadership and in doing so began a five-day discussion that would transform my perspective on leadership styles and institutional cultures. I told them that my talk would be short, as I did not consider myself a "leader." Not that I am incapable of leading, but that I thought leadership in general is grossly overrated. I explained to the group my belief that people rarely need to be led, but instead should be given the opportunity to make decisions for themselves. That true dignity in life comes from self-determination, and when decisions need to be made that affect a group, a simple vote is almost always smarter, wiser, and more just than decisions made by the best "leaders." I went on to explain that most self-professed "leaders" that I have met over the years are pompous narcissists who are motivated more by a desire for power and control than a sense of sincere service or love of others.

It would be weeks later, after the stress of the canyons had faded, that I would come to fully realize the meaning of my unconventional leadership talk. The short talk was less a testimonial about my leadership journey than a diatribe against coercive authority, blind obedience, and unquestioned patterns of thought. Without knowing it at the time, I was revealing the contours of the academic culture in which I was deeply embedded, one in which the quality of ideas, not results or teamwork, are the measure of the person. It is a culture that is inherently individualistic, with professors working in isolation, perfecting ideas, and questioning established ways of thinking. It is a culture in which the attributes of obedience, duty, and loyalty are derided as obstacles to intellectual progress and individual human development.

It is not so much that this cultural perspective is against conventional thinking and assimilation, as it is in favor of individual expression and democratic ideals. The worldview is based on the simple notion that there is something special that can be found in the heart of each person, a light of sorts. From this worldview comes the ethic that things that enable that individual light to shine brightly (e.g., inspirational literature, ground-breaking research, effective teaching, etc.) are viewed as good; things that cast shadows over it are bad. From this perspective, obedience, duty, and loyalty constrain the individual and are viewed with skepticism. Individual reflection, thoughtful deliberation, and a relentless questioning of conventional wisdom are believed to strengthen the light and are viewed as good. Moreover, democratic procedures are preferred to authoritarian rule because they are seen as truly respecting the sanctity of the individual and they aggregate the collective light that is in all of us.

In due time, it was pointed out to me that this worldview, this paradigm in which I operated without thinking, was in stark contrast to the military culture of those around me in the canyon. Military leaders within our group made no apologies for the exercise of authority. For them, military rank was not a privilege to be challenged lightly, but an essential component to establishing order and a vital instrument in achieving common goals. For my new military friends, arriving at camp safely, overcoming physical challenges efficiently, and working as a team are the best measures of leadership, not the number of people who could vote or the extent to which the group adheres to abstract ideals.

Those within this pragmatic, results-oriented, military culture have a profound respect for authority. For them, the attainment of leadership positions is solemn business, appropriate for the most capable members of a group. Exercising power over others is reserved for true leaders, great people who have proven themselves through experience and training, and who possess unquestionable character. This culture is founded on the belief that there are distinct groups of people—those who are qualified and ready to lead and those who are better off being led. Or to continue the earlier metaphor, there are those for whom the light shines brighter and who can serve as guides for others to follow.

Of course, the military culture differs from elitist cultures in that it posits that leadership attributes are not preordained, but that they can be developed over time through experience, indoctrination, and training. Nevertheless, like other class-based cultures, the military culture puts its faith in the wisdom of the leader, rather than the demands of the multitude. Through selfless training, careful study, and sincere deliberation, leaders of the highest character are believed to overcome the chains of self-interest and greed and provide inspirational guidance to those entrusted to them.

Unlike most academic pursuits, which tend to be solitary endeavors, the day-to-day work of the military is teamwork, and military culture is built on the idea that effective teams need effective leaders. From this perspective, the goal of true leadership is not to reflect mass opinion, or even to seek it, but to guide the actions of those under the leaders' command. What is best for achieving the mission of the group is always the central focus.

Unlike the academic culture which has little use and grave distrust for obedience, the military culture gives primacy to the civic virtues that promote active followership. Self-control and duty are guiding principles within all military cultures. The differences between the academic and military cultures are most clearly seen in the competing languages of the two cultures. Military leaders are "trainers" and deliver "briefs." Academics are "educators," give "lectures," and lead "discussions." Military cultures rely on periods of "indoctrination," while academic communities seek to liberate students from their "cultural baggage." The cement that binds a group, according to the military tradition, is formed from a combination of inspirational leaders, wise rules that leaders enact, and a competent and loyal followership. The cement that binds academic communities is a persistent and systematic questioning of existing ideas, especially the ideas of those in positions of authority.

Somewhere between the academic and the military cultures that are outlined here lies a third cultural perspective on ethical leadership, the NOLS culture. At the heart of NOLS culture is what they describe as expedition behavior. Not surprisingly, expedition behavior has characteristics of an academic culture (NOLS after all is an outdoor leadership school) and a military culture (NOLS also stresses leadership development through challenging and sometimes dangerous group activities). From the military side, NOLS stresses duty and commitment to the group. But as a school, NOLS also stresses aspects more commonly associated with academic cultures than military cultures, such as being kind and open-hearted.

Expedition behavior reflects the complexity of NOLS. Like a military organization, NOLS participants overcome a series of physically demanding activities or obstacles (what NOLS collectively refers to as "expeditions" and what a military organization might describe as "operations"). To effectively complete these challenges requires team work, a concern for others, and authentic leadership. In other words, NOLS expeditions require a solid footing in military culture. But unlike the military, the expedition is a means to an end for NOLS participants (a powerful educational tool designed for improving leadership attributes). Stated differently, the military develops leaders to carry out operations and to serve a cause greater than the individual, while NOLS uses expeditions to develop individual leadership attributes. As such, it goes beyond the military culture and takes on additional cultural imperatives.

As was evident throughout the Naval Academy's NOLS expedition, our three cultures had very different group decision-making styles. Those embedded in military culture were most comfortable with the directive and consultative decision-making styles. This occurs when the leader decides and then informs the group or when the leader decides after hearing recommendations from the group. The academics, in contrast, generally viewed consensus as the ideal, but were happy to go with a direct vote if necessary. The NOLS instructors allowed circumstances to determine the decision-making approach. For relatively mundane decisions (e.g., what should be eaten for dinner, should we take time to explore a Native American ruin, is it time for a break), the NOLS instructors were happy to let the group explore their preferred decision-making approaches and to build their leadership muscles. But for big issues, issues that involved safety or that could damage the NOLS reputation, these decisions were made by the NOLS instructors, though they might make efforts to create a modicum of democratic inputs.

These cultural differences revealed themselves during several points throughout the expedition. As mentioned earlier, at the end of day one, the NOLS instructors made the directive decision to move camp after finding the National Monument boundary marker. No long discussions or vote needed. After receiving word from the NOLS instructors, our military friends packed up and moved on without so much as a grumble. At least one academic, yours truly, was slow to move from the preferred location because of a misplaced sign. The maps clearly indicated we were outside of the park boundary and, even if we were not, the current location provided better escape options in the event of flooding. Moreover, I was tired. The lack of meaningful discussion and participant input was a cause of friction for me, but much less so for those within the team-oriented, rule-bound, military culture.

Another cultural conflict was revealed on the second full day of hiking in the canyon. As on the first day, we had hiked much longer and faced challenges that were more physically demanding than anticipated. After another ten-hour hike, this time up Deer Canyon, my leadership group reached a water obstacle that we knew could take a few hours for the entire group to overcome. My group's designated leader for the day, a very capable former Naval Officer who is still very much embedded in Navy culture, gave the order to set up camp, wisely leaving the challenge for the next day.

With our leader investigating the obstacle, our group turned around and looked for the first suitable place to set up camp. Faced with steep canyon walls and no safe place to retreat in the unlikely case that the canyons should flood during the night, we ended up back-tracking a few hundred yards before running into the other leadership teams. Within a few minutes, all three leadership groups were together on the trail (including our NOLS instructors and my group's leader for the day). Some wanted to set up camp where we met (as it was relatively close to the obstacle we would traverse the next morning). My group leader in particular was dismayed that we had already back-tracked more than necessary. Others remembered a comfortable camping spot just a few hundred yards farther back down the canyon and wanted to go back to that site.

With no pressing safety issues at stake or NOLS values in question, the NOLS staff sat back and allowed us to make the decision. But first we had to decide how to make the decision. The easiest method would have been to have the three designated leaders for the day quickly huddle, discuss the situation, and decide where to camp. But undoubtedly, the main point of my previous night's leadership talk was still echoing in the heads of some of my colleagues, and someone suggested that we take a vote. It was wisely decided to have a quick period of discussion before voting, but voting would be the preferred method.

The first person to speak was the designated leader of my group. Though generally a very popular member of our community, his primary argument for staying in the current location focused on his personal need to address bodily functions, but undoubtedly also related to the fact that we had already moved away from the location where he first gave the order to set up camp. Another member of the military community made the argument for backtracking even farther down the canyon, assuring the group that he scouted out an excellent camp location just four minutes down the canyon. We now faced a situation in which two leading members of the military community publicly disagreed, and one of the designated leaders of the day would have their preference overridden by a vote.

We voted to move four minutes down the path and had a relatively restful night, but the experience was quite revealing. Had the person on the losing side of the argument, who was already frustrated with the current situation, been less accepting, had the disagreement turned personal, had the vote dragged on for much longer, things could have ended much differently. Moreover, had the stakes been higher (for example, in an actual military setting), the voting approach could have been disastrous. The incident, and several other key group decision-making events throughout the expedition, left me questioning the essence of my leadership journey. Maybe, just maybe, no one decision-making approach is preferable in all situations. Maybe context, circumstance, and cultural norms should be taken into account when choosing a group decision-making approach. Perhaps we should vote on it!

Ethics Advising a Wells Fargo Whistleblower
A Story of Early Wrongdoing

Thomas E. Creely
U.S. Naval War College

In November 2011, the Episcopal Church Religious Education class engaged the topic of whistleblowing in a lesson on Christian ethics. A businessman in the group stated that blowing the whistle on ethical misconduct was easy. "Just report the unethical actions. What is there to it?" A retired Naval Officer under the alias of Mr. Andrews then asked the question: "Has anyone here ever blown the whistle on ethical misconduct at your work?" There was silence. No one had ever been a whistleblower. Mr. Andrews spoke briefly about the treacherous journey of being a whistleblower and the risks involved. He could speak from first-hand experience, having blown the whistle himself during his time in the Navy.

At the end of the Religious Education class, Naomi (not her real name) approached Mr. Andrews and asked to speak to him. Her questions resulted in an eighteen-month ethics advising relationship with a Wells Fargo teller. This was a pro bono case given her husband's failed business, and they could not afford an attorney. Mr. Andrews told Naomi that he was not able to give legal advice, but could give ethics advice on how to handle the situation. Naomi had never worked where her ethics were challenged to the degree she was experiencing. This was at a local Wells Fargo branch bank as a teller.

Naomi began telling her story of branch leaders disregarding banking procedures and protocols to ensure financial soundness and security. She was disturbed at the blatant and intentionally unorthodox operating style. "What do I do?" she exclaimed in frustration, "I can't just stand by and do nothing while watching this unethical activity occur!"

Mr. Andrews stated up front, "Naomi, being a whistleblower comes with risks. It is not easy! There is no moral courage without costs. You will not be a hero in this story. In fact, you will mostly likely become the pariah and could lose your job."

He listened and tested her motivation for being a whistleblower. Was there disgruntlement? Personal animus? Or was there a real ethical issue for her to deal with? Mr. Andrews quickly learned that she was faced with a legitimate ethics challenge. She asked what her options were, to which he replied, "You have three options, Naomi: 1. You can quit your job, 2. you can remain silent and endure it, or 3. you can take action by reporting the ethical misconduct." He explained the risks with each of the three options from unemployment in a time of financial need, having knowledge of misconduct and doing nothing about it risking employment, and being terminated for reporting the misconduct. Needing time to contemplate the choices and risks, the duo reconvened a few days later by phone.

The issue facing the teller was regular weekly cash deposits she received at her window that ranged between $8,000 and $9,500. Each week, an amount in that range was deposited to a New York bank account. The man would hand the same black bag with cash to the teller for deposit. Opening the bag always emitted the smell of marijuana. She sensed something was wrong about this regular, irregular activity. Mr. Andrews knew this activity was not in keeping with banking regulations.

When Naomi reported this irregular practice to the head teller, she was met with cool dismissiveness. She pressed the head teller on submitting a Suspicious Activity Report (SAR) on the subsequent transactions. The head teller told her, "That is unnecessary. Don't you worry about it. I'll take care of it." Naomi took the issue to the branch manager who dissuaded her from completing a SAR. Like the head teller, the branch manager said he would take care of things and for her not to worry about it.

Federal law requires that a SAR be submitted for irregular occurrence of cash transactions between $8,000 and $10,000. The bank branch manager and head teller were disregarding the law.

The next large cash deposit made by the same man on Thursday at the same time, Naomi took it upon herself to complete the SAR and submitted it online without the support of the head teller and branch manager. When Naomi mentioned to the head teller what she had done, the head teller told her angrily, "That is not the way we do things here. I told you I would take care of it." Naomi's actions put her in the crosshairs of the branch leadership.

The activity continued. Naomi was fearful of continuously receiving suspicious deposits and not reporting them. Again, she approached the branch manager. He told her that he would take care of things and she need not worry. The branch manager and the head teller began to question her work intimidatingly. It was clear that Naomi was not to question the suspicious large deposits.

Almost immediately, innuendos and veiled threats by leaders and other tellers began. This heightened the fear and stress factor for Naomi. She was frustrated at leadership and fearful of consequences. No one would listen to her.

Mr. Andrews later told her, "Naomi, you have responsibility to take this to higher authorities. It appears the head teller and branch manager may be on the take." This really frightened her. He suggested she call the Wells Fargo hotline, which she did. However, the hotline attendant challenged the veracity of her story. She didn't think they believed her.

Mr. Andrews had directed Naomi to take detailed notes and document everything that happened. Her manager began to intimidate her and her fearful stress increased. Yet, she chose to persevere. Mr. Andrews was in disbelief at the disregard for such blatant violations.

How does she get the attention of Wells Fargo leadership? After a lot of thought, Mr. Andrews called a close contact in the intelligence community and told him the story. His contact said it could be narcoterrorism: the selling of drugs in the United States to fund terrorism. Immediately, Mr. Andrews called a Drug Enforcement (DEA) friend, who put him in touch with the financial crimes unit.

Realizing that no one was paying attention to Naomi's concerns, Mr. Andrews' DEA contact decided the best course of action would be for Mr. Andrews to visit the Wells Fargo regional office. Upon arriving, he told the receptionist, "I needed to speak with the senior leadership. No one under a Vice President. Please take these three words to the senior leadership: Narcoterrorism, money laundering and criminal activity at a local Wells Fargo Branch."

She immediately went to the executive suite. A short time later, a Senior Vice President and an Executive Assistant came down. The officer told them Naomi's story about the cash deposits, the intimidation, veiled threats, and fear she was experiencing. As he spoke, they took copious notes. He had their attention. They promised to help and protect Naomi.

Naomi was put in contact with a very helpful Human Resources person. After a few weeks, she was handed off to another HR person who again questioned the veracity of her story. Frustrated, she continued to persevere.

Mr. Andrews' conversations with Naomi continued as he advised her how to deal with other emerging ethical situations. Some of them are what he might call red herrings to distract her from the main issue of money laundering. Vault policies were disregarded, leaving the security of cash at risk, and other procedural shortcuts were taken.

One day out of the blue, Mr. Andrews received an attention-getting email from the Wells Fargo General Counsel in Charlotte, NC. He accused Mr. Andrews of acting as an attorney for Naomi, threatening action against him. This was a moral challenge for Mr. Andrews. He had to evaluate his actions as ethics advisor. These questions popped into his head for rapid ethical analysis: Have I done anything wrong? Is this a threat to intimidate me from giving Naomi ethics advice? Do I back away from such a threat? Or do I defend my position as an ethicist to Naomi? Do I stand with this woman who has the courage to take a stand against Wells Fargo leaders?

After a nice introductory sentence, Mr. Andrews quickly wrote his defense, stating:

> In no way have I given any legal counsel. I am a PhD ethicist, not an attorney.
>
> Naomi has not revealed any names or personally identifiable information of Wells Fargo employees. She has only identified leadership positions, responsibilities, and questionable activities.
>
> As an ethicist, I have the right to advise her to bear moral judgment and responsibility not only for herself, but also as an employee for Wells Fargo.
>
> I am clergy (a retired Navy Chaplain), which allows her privileged communication along with the constitutional guarantee of free speech.

Mr. Andrews hit the send button. Almost immediately he received a response stating, "Thank you for assisting Ms. Naomi with the ethical complexities and for the interests of Wells Fargo." That short twenty-minute exchange was a test of Mr. Andrews' moral will. He chose to stand by Naomi and to stand for his profession as a practicing ethicist.

After a few weeks the police surrounded the branch. All staff were fired except for Naomi. Change was in place. Multiple individuals from another state were brought in by Wells Fargo to take control. Life had settled down. It was a victory for moral courage—or so they thought.

Cross-Selling

A few months later, Naomi called Mr. Andrews asking about other questionable activities occurring at the branch. She told him about employees opening accounts in customers' names without their consent.

Having been a banker in his early life, with two banking and finance degrees, Mr. Andrews was familiar with general banking protocol and procedures. Naomi's description and documentation of cross-selling were not in the best interest of the customers, nor Wells Fargo. Forging signatures, taking legal action without consent of the customer, opening multiple accounts under a name—it certainly did not pass the smell test. Mr. Andrews advised Naomi to collect evidence and document specific events. Once a week Mr. Andrews had breakfast with a group of executives, which included a regional bank ethics officer of a competitor bank. Without disclosing his ethics advising role, he queried him about policies, procedures, and protocols for opening accounts in customers' names without customer knowledge. Without question, the competitor ethics officer stated that it was "absolutely illegal to open accounts in people's names without their consent." Other issues of accountability were discussed. Mr. Andrews reported to Naomi his conversation with the bank ethics officer.

Naomi reported the unethical cross-selling to Human Resources. Again, they doubted her story and believed her to be a chronic whistleblower. Certainly, thoughts of "Is she imagining this," "perhaps she is confused, given it is unquestionably illegal," and "maybe the stress of whistleblowing and her financial situation is bearing upon her" crossed Mr. Andrews' mind. He informed Naomi that the pressure would build on her with another whistleblowing claim. She had better make sure she was right and have impeccable documentation. She persevered, and Mr. Andrews continued to persevere with her.

The new branch leadership team started passive-aggressive behaviors to intimidate, threaten, and weaken her will. Again, she and Mr. Andrews navigated the treacherous ethical landscape. Wells Fargo put pressure on her not to talk with Mr. Andrews even though they continued. Intimidation, veiled threats, and not-so-veiled threats increased by the local branch leaders. They also resorted to what Fred Alford in *Whistleblowers: Broken Lives and Organizational Power* calls "constructive discharge." What do you think constructive discharge means? Word had gotten to the new leadership and tellers that she was a whistleblower. She had "destroyed careers and ruined lives."

It became management's mission to engineer her departure with manufactured charges of misconduct, unethical actions, and procedural violations.

Naomi refused to standby and allow such unethical banking practices to take place.

The incredible stress and pressure along with sleepless nights and fear for her own safety bore heavily on Naomi and her family. She was tiring from the fight, relationships became strained, and the stress was continuing to mount. After some soul-searching, Naomi resigned her teller position from the bank.

This was the high-pressured cross-selling tactics that led to Wells Fargo's current state of affairs with the federal government and the public trust.

The cross-selling scandal. There was tremendous pressure for all employees to fill their daily quota to open new accounts. There were financial incentives for the regional, district, and branch leadership.

The intense demand was for the opening of multiple new accounts for existing customers. How was this accomplished:

1. Convincing customers of bogus benefits.
2. Warning customers of non-existent penalties if they did not open the account.
3. Opening accounts in customers' names without their consent or knowledge.
4. Committing outright deceit by lying to the customer in multiple other ways. Many victims were senior citizens.

This was one the most incentivized, creative, innovative, and systematic ethical misconducts the financial world had seen. It was the Wells Fargo culture of fraud. Bonus incentives, intimidation, and high pressure on managers and employees to get the numbers up appears to have been devoid of any ethical parameters.

Cross-selling banking products is a common marketing strategy for increasing profit and maximizing the customer relationship. Wells Fargo's cross-selling techniques were fraught with fraud. At the hands of Wells Fargo employees, customers suffered costly overdrafts and fees, bad credit ratings, loss of homes and other assets, not to mention a deteriorating trust relationship with Wells Fargo. Naomi had an elderly lady come to the branch to inquire about an unauthorized account. She took the customer's complaint to the manager. The manager told Naomi to lie to the lady. Naomi refused. The manager took it upon himself to speak with the lady and deceive her into opening an account. Some of the employees who reported the unethical behavior to Wells Fargo were met with more than skepticism. It was disbelief and denial.

After resigning, Mr. Andrews heard nothing more from Naomi about Wells Fargo from 2013 until September 2016, when the largest bank scandal of the year made big news. She emailed him: "This is what we were dealing with. Can you believe it!" The Wells Fargo massive consumer fraud was more than they ever imagined. They had thought it was only a local branch problem that had been swept under the carpet. Wells Fargo had swept it and many more under the carpet.

Wells Fargo, third largest bank in the United States, has been in the news for fraudulently cross-selling banking products and other illicit banking and unethical practices since. Both the United States House and Senate excoriated Chairman and Chief Executive Officer John Stumpf for the unethical practices of his bank. Mr. Stumpf has since resigned.

Was it the Wells Fargo culture that led to the fraud or just out-of-control high pressure incentivized selling techniques with no harm intended?

The Wells Fargo Fallout

- Fifty-three hundred employees fired over opening more than three million phony accounts.
- $185 million paid in fines.
- Millions of customers lost homes and cars, have ruined credit ratings, and damaged reputations.
- Allegations of opening accounts in the names of undocumented minority immigrants.
- Facing multiple lawsuits from customers, whistleblowers, and federal and state agencies.

The Wall Street Journal reported that dozens of employees blew the whistle on cross-selling fraud over the course of four years. Many of those stories match Naomi's story.

Ethics advising was important and beneficial to Naomi. It helped her to evaluate her own values, test those values, and examine the world through a new experience. Changing contexts required constant risk analysis. Decisions were left to her. Throughout the eighteen-month experience, Mr. Andrews had to revisit the objectives and where he and Naomi were headed. It required deep analysis, consulting with others, and ensuring that he was giving the best ethical advice.

Here are some questions that Mr. Andrews had to consider as an ethicist advising a whistleblower:

1. Do ethicists play a role in whistleblowing?
2. Are there ethics in whistleblowing that the whistleblower needs to consider?
3. When an employee decides to blow the whistle, are there ethical responsibilities on that employee with the bank?
4. Or is that employee free by any means to report the unethical behavior with the ends justifying the means?

5. How do I engage the whistleblower and other parties?

Realized in the Wells Fargo experience are some ethical whistleblowing axioms to be applied in most whistleblowing scenarios. Risk-Benefit Analysis is essential to a whistleblower's moves. Whistleblowing is not just about the employee and employer—it deeply concerns one's family. It is more than doing the honorable duty of reporting misbehavior. Motives and ends must be considered. There has to be a willingness to suffer ridicule and even be considered a pariah among colleagues and co-workers.

Takeways

Here are some points for ethicists to consider when advising whistleblowers:

1. Whistleblowing is a treacherous path that needs to be well thought out.
2. Point out the personal costs of whistleblowing. Are you taking the right risks for the right reasons? Risk relationships, income, retirement, benefits with children in college?
3. Question your client's motives for blowing the whistle.
4. Remain objective. Look at the different facets of the context and players.
5. Examine the effects whistleblowing will have on family and significant others.
6. Advise the whistleblower that she is not going to be the hero.
7. Differentiate between critical and small misconduct activities. Beware of red herrings.
8. Be aware of biases and changing context.
9. Empower the whistleblower with moral clarity and resources to make sound judgments.
10. Provide the whistleblower appropriate legal, psychological, and spiritual resources. Stress – develop ways of coping.
11. Maintain your own objectivity and professionalism while supporting the whistleblower.
12. Look for an opportunity to hand off the whistleblower to a competent, credible, and honest person of authority.

Ethicists do have moral authority to advise whistleblowers. Don't be intimidated by others exerting their power. Claim your moral authority even when challenged by others.

Note: Names have been changed to protect identities of individuals in this story.

Le Cong Co
A Vietnamese Legacy of Ethical Leadership

James A. Schnell
Fulbright Scholar Association

Abstract

This article examines the legacy of ethical leadership lived by Le Cong Co. His life and career in Vietnam has involved years as an educator, a Viet Cong fighter seeking to eject American military forces from Vietnam, and a Vietnamese government official after the Americans withdrew from Vietnam and educational administration. He presently is the founder, President and Provost of Duy Tan University—the largest private university in central Vietnam.

The ethical dimensions of his leadership are interpreted using four categories of ethical leadership: charismatic ethical leadership, contingent reward ethical leadership, regulatory focus ethical leadership and virtuous ethical leadership. As such, an international understanding of ethical leadership is enhanced via focus on a Vietnamese leader using Vietnamese perspectives on ethical leadership as the basis of interpretation.

Ethical leadership practices often evolve from lives of struggle whereby the individual learns to sharpen innate skills that resonate with those around him/her. Such is the case of Le Cong Co. His is a story that grows out of deep desperation and a will to survive and ultimately prosper.

He grew up in country that was occupied by foreign forces, which had a history of such occupation, and he worked diligently to serve the needs of his family, community and country. He was a teacher, then drawn into military service to repel foreign invaders, served his country militarily with uncommon valor, returned to education after the foreign forces departed and went on to found a university.

That his story would be told favorably in an American publication is ironic because the country he fought so valiantly against was the United States. It is assumed that, with the passage of time, the international community can recognize ethical leadership from all sides of an international controversy. Human beings are not able to dictate the circumstances they are born into. They do have input regarding how they address those circumstances. The life of Le Cong Co exemplifies an impressive array of life choices that reflect significant ethical leadership.

The concept of ethical leadership is defined as "the demonstration of normatively appropriate conduct through personal actions and interpersonal relationships, and the promotion of such conduct to followers through two-way communication, reinforcement, and decision-making" (Brown, Trevino & Harrison, 2005, p. 118). The following four categories of ethical leadership will be used to interpret the ethical leadership qualities of Le Cong Co: charismatic ethical leadership, contingent reward ethical leadership, regulatory focus ethical leadership and virtuous ethical leadership.

Use of the aforenoted four categories is stressed within a Vietnamese contextual understanding presented by Mai Ngoc Khuong and Vo Minh Duc in "The Effect of Ethical Leadership on Employees Virtuous Behavior: A Study of Marketing Agencies in Ho Chi Minh City, Vietnam" (2015, pp. 832–839). Hence, depiction of Vietnamese leadership ethics is enhanced via interpretation using a Vietnamese theoretical frame of reference.

Le Cong Co was born November 28, 1941 in Ai My, Dien Tho, Dien Ban, Quang Nam Province, Vietnam and received his elementary and secondary education in the Viet-Minh region during the second period of Vietnamese resistance against the French colonialists. In 1959, before the age of ten, he joined the war effort after the death of his mother, sister and brother from starvation that occurred in relation to the French occupation of Vietnam. The Viet-Minh, led by Ho Chi Minh, was the Vietnamese resistance movement against the French colonialists. Co served as a scout for the Viet-Minh resistance in Quang Nam Da Nang between 1950–54. This function helped him to gain skills with human relations insofar as learning to interpret fundamental human behaviors.

At the age of fourteen Le Cong Co advanced to the role of messenger for the National Liberation Front, also known as the Viet Cong, in Saigon and served in this capacity until he was eighteen (1959). During this time, he sharpened his insights with motivation and gained an appreciation for the role of ethics in human relations. They actively resisted the dictatorship of Ngo Dinh Diem, who was later killed by pro-American forces. He was also the leader of the anti-war movement, at Chu Van An High School, in Saigon. His graduation from high school in 1958 was distinctive in that he placed second, among 500 high school graduates, in the French style educational system utilized by his high school. He then went on to serve as a high school teacher in Can Tho.

His academic talents were recognized via his completion of a Bachelor of Science degree at the Sorbonne Program (Saigon) in 1963, where he ranked top of his class in the mathematics major. He was offered a scholarship for PhD study in Nuclear Physics at McGill University, Canada but did not pursue this opportunity due to the on-going war effort in Vietnam. However, he did serve as a Lecturer at Hue University for two years (1962–64)—which was one of only two universities in South Vietnam at that time.

His life in academia blended with continued service to his country as they sought to oust foreign forces from Vietnam. Ethical distinctions that contrasted just and unjust governmental actions had very real consequences for his worldview. Between 1960–65, at the ages of nineteen to twenty-four, Le Cong Co was President of the College Student Association in Central Vietnam, Hue. In that capacity he worked as an undercover agent to attract students to support the cause of North Vietnam to unite the country, served as the head of the anti-war student movement at Hue University and collected intelligence information for North Vietnam by working as the tutor for children of a number of top officials of South Vietnam. During this time period he was protected by the Hue Police Chief, who had a brother working as a major colonel of the North Vietnamese Army in Hanoi.

Le Cong Co's skill with organizing capabilities were recognized and he continued his climb into leadership positions. His appreciation for the role of ethics in motivating those he led evolved and his reputation as an ethical leader grew. He served as President of the Da Nang Communist Youth Movement during 1964–65 whereby he built underground insurgent forces serving in Da Nang. "In the early 1960s, it was primarily members of the second generation of political activists emerging from this family (the family of Nguyen Thuc Tuan) who would form the core of Le Cong Co's Youth Association and fill most of leadership positions in Hue" (Lillie, 2014, p. 34)

One of the high points of his leadership during this time was the peaceful takeover of Da Nang City Hall that involved students and workers. It lasted nine days before being suppressed by the South Vietnamese police. His years as an activist were full of such protest actions. He learned to negotiate ethical dilemmas that he encountered and was able to employ lessons learned from such encounters.

Nguyen Thuc Lu brought Le Cong Co to Thanh Luong village in 1961 to work with a group of family, friends and neighbors "who would then go on to become the core leadership of the Youth Association in Hue. During this fateful meeting, Le Cong Co and Nguyen Thuc Lu established the command structure for the organization. Leadership responsibilities for the organization were assigned as follows: Duong Dinh Na was made President of the Youth Association in Hue; Pham Van Duc was assigned the position of Vice President in charge of military affairs; Nguyen Thuc Tan was assigned the position of committee" (Le, 2012, p. 70). This emphasis on rich interpersonal relationships was based on common trust and ethical understanding of one another.

It is worth noting that the motivation for his efforts was to free Vietnam from foreign domination, that was seen to be an unethical international action. Le Cong Co is quoted in that regard by Aaron Lillie.

> "Although originally founded by order of the central leadership of the NLF in Saigon, most students who joined cared little about communism and were principally motivated by a patriotic desire to resist what they viewed as an invasion by a foreign power." (Lillie, 2014 p. 7). Aaron Lille elaborates in reporting "the National Liberation Front was itself deeply divided on the issue of what sort of government should be instituted after the war. As former student activist leader Le Cong Co has pointed out, the student movement in southern Vietnam was 'a patriotic movement, not a communist movement. There were some people in the movement who were communists, but most people were patriots....'" (Lille, 2014, p. 10).

He continued his advancement by becoming a Committee Member of the National Liberation Front of Central Vietnam in 1965. This placed him at the forefront of Viet Cong forces fighting to eject American forces from Vietnam. By 1966, he was President of the Thua Thien Hue Province Communist Youth Movement whereby he built strong ties with the Buddhist resistance movement in Hue, collected intelligence information for North Vietnam, coordinated many strikes and walk-outs at Hue schools and factories, and built underground insurgent forces in Hue. It was during this period he came to better understand ethical orientations as being, not only just, but more effective with the accomplishment of his organizational goals and objectives.

Nguyen Thuc Lu brought a range of individuals together to form a solid cadre of regional student activists who were led by Le Cong Co. "After Lu and Co were introduced by Lu's father Tuan they had quickly become close friends while attending Hue University. Together the two of them set about building the foundations of an organization that would eventually grow to several hundred students spread out over a five-province area of central Vietnam" (Le, 2012, p. 70).

> Le Cong Co's leadership and ethical insights with Vietnamese politics enhanced his ability to assess developments related to U.S. intervention in Vietnam. Aaron Lille writes "According to the former President of the Youth Association in central Vietnam, Le Cong Co, 'one of the biggest mistakes the Americans made was assassinating Ngo Dinh Diem. After the fall of the Diem regime there was no government that could rival it, and because of that, the Americans had to pour troops into southern Vietnam to save the government'" (Lille, 2014, p. 44).

Co's understanding for how interpersonal and international ethical dimensions had parallels became sharper during this period and he grew in his ability to apply this understanding.

In 1967 Le Cong Co was named political chief for Battalion 810, North Vietnamese Army. During that time his cover was blown in Da Nang while disembarking an airplane at the Da Nang airport. A gunfight ensued at the airport and he was almost caught by South Vietnamese Secret Services at the airport. This resulted in him going into the jungles, and he was promoted to lead Battalion 810 of the North Vietnamese Army in Thua Thien Hue. Co credits his ability to detect his blown cover and avoid capture to sensitivities with the human condition that he developed via a growing appreciation for ethical dynamics associated with deceptions practiced by his opposition.

By that time the Viet Cong were preparing for the Tet Offensive in 1968. During the Tet Offensive, Le Cong Co led Battalion 810, which was assigned to capture the ancient palace in Hue. His unit hung a large Vietnamese National Liberation Front flag on top of the ancient palace in Hue. The flag's posting lasted for twenty-five days of fierce fighting against American, South Korean, and South Vietnamese forces. This led to ferrying wounded North Vietnamese soldiers across the Perfume River when they were driven out of Hue by American forces. The Tet Offensive battles in Hue are depicted in the American film "Full Metal Jacket."

The Kokava Campaign, Asao–Aluoi Thua Thien Hue followed within which they battled against twenty American battalions across eighteen hills in Asao and Aluio. This event is depicted in the American film "Hamburger Hill." He was promoted to the rank of Major Colonel, at the age of twenty-eight, as result of the Kokava Campaign. Later the same year, he led Viet Cong forces in the Da Bac Battle (Silver Stone Battle) at Thua Thien Hue. They attacked the stronghold of American forces in Da Bac, sustained significant casualties due to false intelligence from the scout battalion about the layout of American defenses in Da Bac and captured some American troops resulting in acquisition of an American map that guided the Viet Cong through the artillery fire of American forces.

The fighting against the Viet Cong and Americans was exceedingly intense, brutal and raw. According to Le Cong Co:

> Surviving the combined American and RVN onslaught in the jungle and countryside around Hue over next four years was as much a matter of luck as anything else....People didn't understand how I was still alive because the fighting was so fierce....Other people went on missions. They all died. The entire group that was with me all died, only I survived....There were some days when I was in Phu Van that tanks demolished all of the houses and underground hideouts. Some days 50–70 guerillas died in one day. (Lille, 2014, pp. 69–70)

Co survived encounters that demanded immediate assessment of other people and their motivations, friend and foe alike, and such assessments drew from and added to his raw understanding of human influence and ethical correlations. Misreading such encounters could equate with instant death.

During the 1970–71 period Le Cong Co was assigned as Political Chief of Regiment Six in Thua Thien Hue. This involved promotion to lead Regiment Six, Division 324B Ngu Binh and many subsequent battles along the Ho Chi Minh Trail. He was promoted to Administrative Chief of the National Liberation Front in Thua Thien Hue in 1972 and guided planning for many North Vietnamese Army campaigns in Thua Thien Hue. He was sent back into Hue in 1972 to lead underground insurgent forces after the collapse of many insurgent cells due to the capture of their leader by South Vietnamese Secret Services. This assignment lasted until 1975 and involved his re-organizing the anti-war student movement in Hue.

During the Paris Peace Treaty Negotiations preparations (1973–74) he was nominated as one of the Vietnamese leaders of the National Liberation Front to participate in the negotiation of the Paris Peace Treaty that involved four entities: the United States, the North Vietnamese government, the South Vietnamese government and the National Liberation Front of

Vietnam. He was sent back to Hue in the middle of the negotiation to prepare for the capture of Hue.

The 1975 liberation of Hue was eventful. Le Cong Co directed the plan involving creation of fear and confusion among the South Vietnamese Army in Hue by having local insurgents dress as civilians and run around the city in chaos, faking evacuation. He received intelligence in early March 1975 from a French Catholic priest that the South Vietnamese Army would retreat from Hue to set up defenses in Da Nang. He reported this to the Hanoi Chief of Staff and helped direct most of the attack by the North Vietnamese Army against the defenses in Da Nang. Le Cong Co led local insurgents to liberate Hue city March 25, 1975 and welcomed the North Vietnamese Army regulars into Hue on the following day.

His work with the liberation of Hue involved welcoming top leaders of North Vietnam to Hue including Communist Party Secretary Le Duan, General and Chief of Staff Võ Nguyen Giap, and Vice Premier To Huu. He personally briefed Communist Party Secretary Le Duan about battlefield conditions and was chosen to become one of the top leaders of the interim government in central Vietnam if the North would have failed to capture Saigon in the move to reunify the country.

The departure of the Americans, and the cessation of related military activities, resulted in Le Cong Co's return to educational interests in Vietnam. He was appointed to head the Hue University system via his promotion to General Secretary of Hue University, the second largest university system in South Vietnam. In that capacity he handled public relations with intellectuals and the common people in Hue.

Between 1976–78 Le Cong Co was a Senior Scholar at the Nguyen Ai Quoc School of Political Science in Hanoi. This position was intended to prepare him for assignment as one of the top leaders in Vietnam. During that time he was offered assignment to South America, to help with the communist movement there, but he declined that opportunity because he did not agree with the plan. He spent some time assessing the scope of his achievements up to that point and gave consideration for how his future service to Vietnam could benefit the country. An enhanced understanding of ethical dynamics was part of that assessment.

The following three years (1978–81) was a turbulent time for Le Cong Co. He was suspended from all political activities in Hanoi and Da Nang and charged with being a proponent of capitalist ideologies and suspicion of being a CIA agent because of his many escapes from near-death situations while working undercover in Da Nang and Saigon during the war. He was sent back to Da Nang for investigation within the formal court system. During that time, a book entitled *Tuition Paid By Blood*, focusing on Le Cong Co as the main character, was published. It was authored by renowned writer Nguyen Khac Phuc and poet Thu Bon. Co believes much of his defense was grounded in application of ethical leadership principles, both on his part and the part of those investigating him.

He was cleared of all charges in 1981 after 30,000 pages of documents were located in the U.S. Embassy in Saigon that detailed various U.S. activities in Vietnam. He was then assigned to handle relations with overseas Vietnamese. This position involved travel to Eastern Europe to study about various successful models of communism. After a trip to Eastern Europe, Russia and East Germany he wrote an article titled "Communism Will Collapse in Eastern Europe" based on his observations. He was disciplined for publishing such an opinion and was almost put on trial for stressing that view.

Controversy surrounding publication of *Tuition Paid in Blood* erupted in 1983 in relation to information presented in the book. The Vietnamese Politburo suspended publication of the book and an inquiry ensued. There was public criticism of the book and copies of it were burnt in protest in Hue. He was subject to direct discipline by Vice-Premier To Huu. Similarly, a book about Le Cong Co titled *City in Windfall* was published in 1985 but was banned in Hue.

He served as a Senator in Hanoi between 1986–1992. He ran for office independently, without nomination support by the Vietnamese Communist Party, and became the first independent candidate in the modern history of Vietnam to win a seat in the Senate. He believes his reputation for having a sterling ethical foundation was key in his being elected/re-elected and serving with distinction.

He exercised influence during the "Doi Moi" period in Vietnam that stressed renovation of the Vietnamese economy as it transitioned from a central-planning economic model to a market-oriented economic model. This involved writing the new Investment Law in Vietnam. He also input clauses for the new Education Law which included establishment of private universities and colleges. Part of his team changed the Constitution of Vietnam whereby China was removed from the list of arch enemies, freedom rights for citizens were established and the Senate was set up as an independent organization that functions separately from the central government.

By that point, Le Cong Co's career had evolved from educator, to activist, to soldier, to politician. He then returned to his first occupational domain, education, and pursued innovations having to do with educational institutions in Vietnam. His first significant educational venture in this period emphasized creation of Central Vietnam University in 1986. This venture failed when it's proposed establishment was rejected by Prime Minister Do Muoi.

He was elected to committee membership in The National Scholar Association of Vietnam in 1987. That membership continued for over thirty years and involved many terms. In 1988, he created the Center of Practical English in Da Nang. It was the first private training center in Vietnam and attracted thousands of students to study English. Later the same year, he opened the Center of Electronics & Informatics Technologies in Da Nang. It was the first private center to study about these fields in Vietnam.

Le Cong Co served as the Head of Tourism & Hospitality of Quang Nam in Da Nang between 1988–92. During this period he built the Furma Resort as the first inland five-star hotel in Vietnam. It was modeled after the floating five-star hotel in Saigon. He also contributed to development of the Cross-Indochina road running from Vietnam to Laos to Thailand.

Le Cong Co took a distinct step with his vision of educational innovation by establishing Duy Tan University in 1992. It is located in Da Nang. He has served as president and provost. The path for founding the institution evolved through his re-application for the establishment of the Central Vietnam University, that had been rejected earlier. However, this re-application was accepted contingent on the name being changed to Duy Tan University and a cap on the number of students being set at five hundred.

Since 1992, Duy Tan University has grown and become well-recognized in Vietnam. It is presently ranked the number one private university in Vietnam and ranked number nine among all universities in country. Enrollment has grown to over 22,000. Innovation has been a key factor for the university. It received permission to offer graduate programs in 2008, it is one of the ten Vietnamese universities granted permission to offer online programs and it has academic partnerships with well-known universities in the U.S. (including Carnegie Mellon University, Penn State, California State University/Fullerton and the University of North Carolina). He has served as the Vice-President, Association of Private Universities of Vietnam since 2004.

Le Cong Co's involvement with higher education in Vietnam is based on an exceptional public service career that has transcended teaching, military service, government service and educational administration. He believes his reputation for practicing ethical principles has been key to his foundation, personally and professionally. Recognition for his service above self is exemplified in the many honors that have been bestowed upon him. He received the National War Hero Medal in 1971 for his work with the National Liberation Front of Vietnam (however the award was later revoked in relation to political issues) and the Medal of National Independence in 1995 (for war time achievements). He is also listed in the Official Book of Historic Persons in Vietnam, which officially recognizes him as one of the historic persons in modern day Vietnam. In 2016 he was granted National Labor Hero status in relation to his efforts after the American war as politician and educator.

The contributions of Le Cong Co and his comrades have received overdue recognition in recent years as the relevance of their achievements is recognized.

Le Cong Co and a community of Vietnamese scholars centered around Duy Tan University, working in collaboration with historian Ngo Vinh Long, have been steadily building up a body of Vietnamese language scholarship on the history of National Liberation Front-led student organizations. This has resulted in the publication of a number of Vietnamese language historical texts and other materials related to the student movement, including books, academic articles and film and television documentaries. As yet, none of this material has been translated into English, and very little has been scrutinized by scholars outside of Vietnam. (Lillie, 2014, p. 76)

Co and his comrades consistently stress the role of ethical variables in understanding how they persevered and thrived in times of hardship and sacrifice.

The following four categories of ethical leadership can be used to interpret the ethical leadership qualities of Le Cong Co: charismatic ethical leadership, contingent reward ethical leadership, regulatory focus ethical leadership and virtuous ethical leadership. Illustrations for each category will be offered from perspectives he has conveyed. Use of the aforenoted four categories is stressed within a Vietnamese contextual understanding presented by Mai Ngoc Khuong and Vo Minh Duc in "The Effect of Ethical Leadership on Employees Virtuous Behavior: A Study of Marketing Agencies in Ho Chi Minh City, Vietnam" (2015, pp. 832–39). Hence, depiction of Vietnamese leadership ethics is enhanced via interpretation using a Vietnamese theoretical frame of reference.

Charismatic Ethical Leadership

According to Brown & Trevino (2005, p. 956) charismatic ethical leadership is defined as when "inspirational leaders who convey ethical values, are other-centered rather than self-centered, and who role model ethical conduct." Le Cong Co refers to this type of phenomena when he speaks of love for oneself, fellow citizens and country. He recognizes love as the root of ambition, passion and patriotism. He stresses that love, career and country are the three elements connecting our lives together. Co believes this will culminate with mutual benefit for ourselves and others.

Contingent Reward Ethical Leadership

The concept of contingent reward ethical leadership is defined as "an exchange of rewards between leaders and followers in which effort is rewarded by providing rewards for good performance or threats and disciplines for poor performance" (Muenjohn, 2008, p. 6). The Vietnamese cultural context is evident with emphasis on this domain in that Le Cong Co bluntly states Vietnamese will not be successful in their careers if their nation is invaded. This is with reference to Vietnam being invaded by the U.S., the French before that, the Japanese before that and the Chinese before that.

He summarizes lessons from the Vietnam-American war years using the key objectives that motivated him: 1) reunification of the country; 2) freedom from foreign domination; 3) alleviating oppression, poverty and disadvantage. Hence, these were rewards he was seeking to achieve at that time and are foundation for what he presently stresses.

Regulatory Focus Ethical Leadership

Regulatory Focus Ethical Leadership "has two components, which are ethical promotion focus and ethical prevention focus." (Shao, 2010, p. 79). That is, in some instances we can promote ethical objectives while, in other instances, we can better realize ethical objectives via prevention of some behaviors. He cautions that the ethics of the younger generation are being negatively influenced and, in some ways, we don't understand that we are slowly losing their potential. This is followed up with the belief that caring and sharing with others will make our lives more tranquil.

Virtuous Ethical Leadership

The concept of virtuous ethical leadership is defined as leading with "behaviors beneficial to others that reflect moral ideals and involve personal costs or risks. Virtuous ethical behaviors are praiseworthy if performed and not blameworthy if not performed" (Trevino, Brown & Hartman, 2003,

p. 10). Such positions are manifested in the Duy Tan University principles and doctrine.

The Duy Tan University principles are to teach and learn by following humanistic principles. Graduates should be sympathetic and willing to help the underprivileged. Duy Tan University doctrine stresses building a teaching and research university based on the foundation of humanitarianism and innovation and to educate global citizens with moral qualities and community awareness.

One might think there would be ill feelings on the part of the Vietnamese against the U.S. but that is not the case. Le Cong Co, during a 2013 interview, offered his thoughts on how the Vietnamese-American War occurred against the desires of the Vietnamese and Americans.

> American participation in the War was a mistake. Indeed America was a not a country that wanted to conquer Vietnam. To Americans, the main issue in Asia was the Chinese. That is the balance of powers, not just in Southeast Asia and Asia, but globally. The Vietnamese- American War occurred against the desires of the Vietnamese and American people." (Lillie, 2014, p. 78)

Co credits his extensive appreciation for relevant ethical perspectives, both Vietnamese and American, helped him to arrive at such a conclusion.

References

Brown, M. E. and L. K. Trevino, "Socialized Charismatic Leadership, Values Congruence, and Deviance in Work Groups," *Journal of Applied Psychology*, vol. 91, no. 4, pp. 954–62, July 2006.

Brown, M. E.; Trevino, L. K. and D. A. Harrision, "Ethical leadership: A social learning perspective for construct development and testing," *Organizational Behavior and Human Decision Processes*, vol. 97, no. 2, pp. 117–34, July 2005.

Le Cong Co, *Nam Thang Dang Nguoi Hoi Ky Volume 1*. Da Nang: Nha Xuat Ban Tre Dai Hoc Duy Tan, 2012.

Lillie, A. *Vietnam's Forgotten Revolutionaries: Student Voices from Inside the Vietnamese Revolution, 1954–1975*. Unpublished M.A. Thesis. University of Washington, 2014.

Mai Ngoc Khuong and Vo Minh Duc. "The Effect of Ethical Leadership on Employee's Virtuous Behavior: A Study of Marketing Agencies in Ho Chi Minh City, Vietnam," *Journal of Economics, Business and Management*, vol. 3, no. 9, September 2015, pp. 832–39.

Muenjohn, N. "Evaluating the Structural Validity of The Multifactor Leadership Questionnaire (MLQ), Capturing The Leadership Factors of Transformational-Transactional Leadership," *Contemporary Management Research*, vol. 04, no. 1, pp. 3–14, March 2008.

Shao, P. "Ethics-Based Leadership and Employee Ethical Behavior: Examining the Mediating Role of Ethical Regulatory Focus," PhD dissertation, Drexel University, PA, 2010.

Trevino, L. K.; Brown, M; and L. P. Hartman, "A Qualitative Investigation of Perceived Executive Ethical Leadership: Perceptions from Inside and Outside of the Executive Suite," *Human Relations*, vol. 56, no. 1, pp. 5–37, Jan. 2003.

Why Ethical Leadership Matters
A Case Study to Improve Military Specialists' Employee Retention Rates

David J. Kritz
National Intelligence University

Background

In 2014, I completed my dissertation that focused on retention issues of military intelligence specialists. These specialists were in the US Air Force as airborne cryptologic language analysts. For the remainder of this paper, the airborne cryptologic language analysts will be referred to as specialists. I used a phenomenological research design to gain a deeper understanding of why the specialists left the military. As I am now an educator who studies and teaches ethics, I believe that my findings can be used as a case study for both leadership practitioners and academics. This article adds to the limited body of research that focuses on ethical leadership or lack thereof affecting employee retention rates. The findings from my study transcend multiple job sectors and may promote the need for ethical leadership.

Introduction

Employee turnover negatively affects for-profit, nonprofit, and U.S. government organizations including the military. Employee turnover raises employee recruitment and training costs and conversely lowers employee morale, job satisfaction, and customer's perceptions of service quality (Cho, Johanson, & Guchait, 2009; Cloutier, Felusiak, Hill, & Pemberton-Jones, 2015). Employee loss can cost a company up to one and a half times the employee's annual income from loss of productivity, loss of tacit knowledge, and the time taken to train a new employee to a level of proficiency compared to the employee who left the company (Saradhi & Palshikar, 2011). Leaders attempting to increase their competitive advantage through intangible assets and globalization also have placed emphasis on employee retention (Longo & Mura, 2011). Further, the decisions of employees who quit yield psychological consequences for the individual and economic consequences for the organization through the probability of increased work stress and unfinished work practices (Proudfoot, Corr, Guest, & Dunn, 2009).

Employee turnover is a human issue that can be mitigated through effective leadership. Thinking about how leadership is practiced is important, as the leaders' decisions and actions directly affect their followers. Leaders who better understand why employees decide to leave an organization may save businesses millions of dollars and lost productivity (Lee & Way, 2010). After developing a strategy on what style of leadership is needed to meet employee expectations, the next step is becoming a leader-practitioner. Leaders who implement an effective leadership style increase the success level of all types of companies (Galli & Muller-Stewens, 2012). Leaders who treat their employees with respect and dignity may achieve a competitive advantage by retaining their star talent and saving capital. Researchers discovered that employees are more committed to an organization when they are treated fairly (Huhtala, Kangas, Lamsa, & Feldt, 2013; Trevino & Weaver, 2003). Ethical leadership may improve the work environment and employee retention rates by treating employees in a fair and just manner.

The simply stated question "What is ethical leadership?" demands a complex response, and rightfully the response should be complex as ethics applies to humans, and humans are adaptive actors. My argument here is that unlike problems that are either simple or complicated, complex issues are difficult to solve because they do not have one root cause. "Ethical leadership is the demonstration of normatively appropriate conduct through personal actions, and interpersonal relationships, and the promotion of such conduct to followers through two-way communication, reinforcement, and decision-making" (Brown, Trevino, & Harrison, 2005, 120). Researchers here argued that the core of effective leadership is comprised of ethical behavior for long-term impact (Bedi, Alpaslan, & Green, 2015; Toor & Ofori, 2009). A personal morality from the leader should be demonstrated for subordinates as a model to follow (Palmer, 2009). Ethical leadership is especially important as it provides a framework for employees to conduct business with each other and reinforces positive behaviors. Ethical leadership exhibits "a fundamental respect for those being motivated to act" (Palmer, 2009, 531). Further, ethical leadership promotes ethical conduct by practicing and consciously managing ethics and ensuring everyone within the organization is held accountable (Toor & Ofori, 2009; Treviño & Brown, 2004). Benefits from ethical leadership include higher levels of job satisfaction, and lower levels of counterproductive work behaviors (Bedi et al.,

2015). Leaders are essential toward ensuring that ethical practices are not only applied, but are intrinsic within an organizational culture. Further, actions of top management, actions of supervisors, and actions of coworkers were three indices of ethics in the workplace used in the National Business Ethics Survey conducted in America to address the relationship between self-organization, ethical fit, and satisfaction (Coldwell, Billsberry, van Meurs, & Marsh, 2008). These three indices of ethics in the workplace are crucial at all levels when it comes to the Department of Defense and national security issues.

Why the Department of Defense (DoD)?

Retaining star talent is important and especially paramount when it comes to defending the nation. Intelligence professionals are one group within the DoD who defend the nation. Within the United States, 4.2 million individuals possess a security clearance for intelligence work (Young, 2013). One facet of military intelligence includes the airborne cryptologic language analysts. These specialists are responsible for protecting national security interests by operating, analyzing, and managing signals intelligence and operations activity. Security ethics is often covered when discussing the Just War, and commonly referred to in Latin as *jus ad bellum*. "The value of security is linked to the value of life and disvalue of violence and injury" (Sorell, Guelke, & Hadjimatheou, 2017, 1). Just War Theory has capability implications for leaders to understand both leadership and ethics. Retaining these intelligence specialists are crucial for decision makers as they provide fidelity to address security concerns by filling previously unknown knowledge gaps. Their work helps leaders make more informed decisions.

In the military, subordinates are expected to follow the orders of their seniors. This guide of followership is specifically written in the Oath of Enlistment (an oath that all individuals who want to join the military must take prior to enlistment). If trust is the currency of leadership, there is then an expectation that leaders will treat their subordinates with ethical standards and moral conduct. Ethics is a strong companion to trust, and provides the foundation of an individual's character (Gensler, 2015). "When you think about what goes into military professionalism, frequently the first word that comes to peoples' mind is ethics" (Klein, 2014, 1). However, what are the implications when the leader acts in an unethical manner?

A Business Ethics Survey cited the following key factors that are most likely to cause individuals to compromise ethical behavior: pressure to meet unrealistic business objectives/deadlines; desire to further one's career; desire to protect one's livelihood; working in an environment with cynicism or diminished morale; and improper training/ignorance that the act was unethical (Hamrog & Forcade, 2006). There is a perception that military leaders place emphasis on competence over character, and now there is an effort to help correct the imbalance (Allen, 2015). When ethical leadership wanes, the leader's actions and decisions may negatively affect an organization that may take decades to correct. Between 2001 and 2015, "The Army vice chief of staff has issued 100 memoranda of reprimand, 147 memoranda of concern and conducted 45 verbal counselings of general officers for myriad behaviors contrary to good order and discipline in the Army" (Allen, 2015, 69). The Army made strides in correcting leadership issues over the fourteen-year period. In some instances, leaders may not understand how their actions and decisions affect their employees. The below study may be used as a case to demonstrate how ethical leadership may improve retention issues.

The Study

While there are numerous negative aspects that derive from employee turnover, it is hard to argue a more serious consequence than those relied upon to help defend the nation. The obstacles toward effective warning to include overcoming enemy deception remain relatively unexplored (Zegart, 2012). Employee turnover is negatively affecting the airborne cryptologic language analysts' career-field, as they had an approximate 25% retention rate within Air Force intelligence organizations once the member's first-term contract was complete (Kritz, 2014). Employee loss affects the Air Force as they help shape the U.S.'s ability to collect and distribute intelligence (Young, 2013).

Four major themes emerged from the airborne specialists' retention study: (a) not optimizing employee skills, (b) poor organizational culture, (c) employee perception of uncaring leadership, and (d) poor job satisfaction (Kritz, 2014). Phenomenology was used as a research method to help gain a deeper understanding of the reasons the airborne specialists left their career-field. Twenty participants (ten male and ten female) who left the career-field for at least five years prior to the study answered semi-structured questions.

Not optimizing the analysts' skills was the most common detriment of job satisfaction. Sixty percent of the participants stated their language skills were underutilized. Participants perceived they were not given an opportunity to effectively use their trained language, and stated that they wanted to have a career that allowed them to reach their full potential. The participants also struggled to maintain language proficiency as they perceived there were organizational obstacles that hampered their effort.

A poor organizational culture was the second theme discovered. The participants stated mistreatment, busywork, not knowing or seeing their supervisors due to deployments were all factors that created a poor organizational culture and were determining factors in employee retention. Twenty percent of the participants wanted to have a stable family life. Fifteen percent of the participants experienced burn out from the workload and having too many responsibilities. The participants also served during the period (between 1993 and 2011) when the Department of Defense Directive 1304.26 (Don't Ask, Don't Tell) policy was the official policy to military members. Five percent of the participants left the career-field because they either wanted to have a relationship or get married to someone of the same sex. Further, the participants stated lack of engagement and the idea of not belonging to a team as invariant constituents when they described the organizational culture.

The participants' understanding of leadership was the third theme. The management style of an organization affects employee turnover when unfair management practices, frequent policy changes, and a hostile work environment occur within the work environment (Yang, Wan, & Fu, 2012). The results revealed that 35% of the participants thought that leadership was poor and uncaring. Twenty percent of the participants stated lack of quality leadership was the reason they decided to leave their career field. Applied leadership is not simply an act, but a continuous process. An essential part of being an effective leader consists of developing and maintaining an affective connection (Palmer, 2009).

The fourth theme was low job satisfaction. Previous researchers found four organizational factors that affect turnover including lifework, job support, salary/benefits, and job satisfaction (Williams et al., 2010). Forty percent of the participants mentioned poor job satisfaction as primary reason for leaving the career field. Fifteen percent of the participants stated having job satisfaction as a favorable condition for career retention. Five percent of the participants mentioned poor job satisfaction as a barrier for influencing the analysts to stay in the career field. An additional 40% of the participants resonated with this common theme. Employee perceptions of organizational work-life support affect organizational commitment, organizational citizenship behaviors, job satisfaction, mental well-being, decreased work–family conflict, and turnover intentions (Valcour et al., 2011).

Implications

Employee turnover causes many negative consequences affecting the departing employee, the remaining employees who remain within the organization, and the leaders. The implication for positive social change includes the potential to assist organizations to establish retention strategies to preserve specialized employees. Further, leaders and managers within an organization will gain new insight toward applying ethical leadership. Leaders who exercise leadership theory may challenge negative states of emotion and tip the balance of an individual who wants to leave the job. Positive relationships were found in previous research between follower's perceptions of ethical leadership and attitudes associated with the leader, including affective trust in the leader, honesty, receiving fair treatment, leader effectiveness, and leadership satisfaction that then correlated to employee loyalty (Bedi et al., 2016; Lee & Way, 2010; & Williams et al., 2010). It appears that ethical leadership mitigates retention issues after analyzing the results from the airborne specialists' retention study. The outcomes from this study could help provide a better understanding of what makes for effective leadership.

Determining processes for maintaining human capital is essential for an organization to maintain talent, keep tacit knowledge, and the means to reduce spending on training new employees fulfilling vacant positions. As effective leadership is a continuous process, so too is process refinement for managers. Like most complexities that involve people, leadership is often the component to settle concerns. Employees value leaders who can change the work atmosphere (Walumbwa, Wu, & Orwa, 2008). The behavioral approach is another aspect worthy of consideration. The behavioral approach theory suggests that followers are much more interested in what leaders' do versus the qualities they possess (Yassir & Mohamad, 2016). This argument places an increased emphasis on an individual's character than on competence. Leaders can change their behaviors if the want is present.

Ways that positively affect employees' mindsets toward organizations include adequate training, an autonomous work environment, and a supportive supervisor (Valcour, Ollier-Malaterre, Matz-Costa, Pitt-Catsouphes, & Brown, 2011). At the senior leader level of the military, the former Defense Secretary Chuck Hagel acted by appointing Rear Admiral Margaret Klein as his Special Advisor for Military Professionalism and "to report directly to him on issues related to military ethics, character, and leadership . . . and competence in all activities at all levels of command . . . [as] a top priority for DoD's senior leadership" (Hagel, 2014, 1).

Theories are effective to help us understand an issue and then grapple with critical thinking that may produce a solution. In this case, affective events theory adds insight to the factors that either motivate or demotivate an individual in the workplace. Affective events theory is evident when work events affect and alter an individual's emotional state (Panaccio & Vandenberghe, 2012). Leaders who create a work environment promoting affective commitment can be done by forming strong employee-supervisor relationships. As affective commitment causes an emotional attachment to the target, supervisors can also experience the desire to strengthen the relationship with the employees who seek mentorship based on connection (Landry & Vandenberghe, 2012). Affective commitment may mitigate retention issues as the airborne specialists perceived their leadership as uncaring. Unfortunately for many employees, the perception of uncaring leaders is not unique to the airborne specialists.

Conclusion

Previous research on employee loss within the airborne cryptologic language analysts' career field found four main emerging themes that caused retention loss which were (a) not optimizing employee skills, (b) poor organizational culture, (c) employee perception of uncaring leadership, and (d) poor job satisfaction (Kritz, 2014). As the airborne specialists' retention rates declined, the tasks the specialists were responsible for did not. More responsibility was bestowed to junior people. "Ethical leadership can fail when it is centered upon a mission that is inherently unsupportable" (Palmer, 2009, 533). My argument is that this case was more unsustainable for long-term execution than it was unsupportable. Additional tasks and responsibilities were thrust on junior (both in age and experience) specialists as the others transitioned out of the military. What is inarguable is that airborne specialists left the community because they perceived they were not treated well within the organization.

Researchers discovered that the importance of studying ethics and leadership improved the central understanding of leadership (Ciulla, 2001; & Huhtala et al., 2013). Employees may be treated better in the work environment as leader practitioners, and academics continue to improve their understanding of leadership. The results from the phenomenological study may be used as a case to ponder the implications of ethical leadership toward the betterment of employee treatment. Further, the themes are not unique to the intelligence community nor the U.S. government. Employee retention issues will occur without applied leadership theory. At first, star talent will leave as they realize their employment opportunities outside the organization. Great employees will leave the organization, and so will good workers. Careers that have the privilege and the burden of dealing with intelligence need talented people to defend the nation. Learning from the retention issues that the intelligence specialists experienced transcends across job sectors to include for-profit, nonprofit, and the military.

References

Allen, C. D. 2015. Ethics and Army leadership: Climate matters. *Parameters; Carlisle Barracks,* 45: 69–83.

Bedi, A., Alpaslan, C. M., & Green, S. 2016. A meta-analytic review of ethical leadership outcomes and moderators. *Journal of Business Ethics,* 139 (3): 517–536. http://dx.doi.org/10.1007/s10551-015-2625-1.

Brown, M., Trevino, L., & Harrison, D. 2005. Ethical leadership: A social learning perspective for construct development and testing. *Organizational Behavior and Human Decision Processes,* 97 (2): 117–134. doi:/10.1016/j.obhdp.2005.03.002.

Cho, S., Johanson, M. M., & Guchait, P. 2009. Employees intent to leave: A comparison of detriments of intent to leave versus intent to stay. *International Journal of Hospitality Management,* 28: 374–381. doi:10.1016/j.jhm.2008.10.007.

Ciulla, J. B. 2001. Carving leaders from the warped wood of humanity. *Canadian Journal of Administrative Sciences,* 18 (4): 313–319.

Cloutier, O., Felusiak, L., Hill, C., & Pemberton-Jones, E. 2015. The importance of developing strategies for employee retention. *Journal of Leadership, Accountability and Ethics,* 12 (2): 119–129. Retrieved from https://search.proquest.com/docview/1726791378?accountid=10504.

Coldwell, D. A., Billsberry, J., van Meurs, N., & Marsh, P. J. G. 2008. The effects of person-organization ethical fit on employee attraction and retention: Towards a testable explanatory model. *Journal of Business Ethics,* 78 (4): 611–622. http://dx.doi.org/10.1007/s10551-007-9371-y.

Dion, M. 2012. Are ethical theories relevant for ethical leadership? *Leadership & Organization Development Journal,* 33 (1): 4–24. http://dx.doi.org/10.1108/01437731211193098.

Gensler, A. 2015. Trust is the most powerful currency in business. *Forbes,* July, 28, 2015. Retrieved from http://fortune.com/2015/07/28/trust-business-leadership/.

Hagel, C. 2014. Statement by Secretary of Defense Chuck Hagel announcing his senior advisor for military professionalism, *US Department of Defense,* March 25, 2014. Retrieved from http://www.defense.gov/Releases/Release.aspx?ReleaseID=16599.

Hamrog, J. J., & Forcade, J. W. 2006. The ethical enterprise: Doing the right things in the right ways, today and tomorrow: A global study of business ethics, *American Management Association*. Retrieved from https://www.amanet.org/images/hrethicssurvey06.pdf.

Huhtala, M., Kangas, M., Lamsa, A., Feldt, T. 2013. Ethical managers in ethical organizations? The leadership-culture connection among Finnish managers. *Leadership & Organization Development Journal*, 34 (3): 250–270. doi:10.1108/01437731311326684.

Klein, M. D. 2014. Statement by Senior Advisor for Military Professionalism Margaret Klein, Ethics advisor equates professionalism with Leadership. *US Department of Defense*, May 15, 2014. Retrieved from http://archive.defense.gov/news/newsarticle.aspx?id=122269.

Kritz, D. J. 2014. *Increasing the airborne cryptologic language analyst career retention rate through applied leadership* (Order No. 3642788). Available from ABI/INFORM Global; ProQuest Dissertations & Theses Global. (1609406065). Retrieved from https://search.proquest.com/docview/1609406065?accountid=10504.

Landry, G., & Vandenberghe, C. 2012. Relational commitments in employee-supervisor dyads and employee job performance. *The Leadership Quarterly*, 23: 293–308. doi:10.1016/j.leaqua.2011.05.016.

Lee, C., & Way, K. 2010. Individual employment characteristics of hotel employees that play a role in employee satisfaction and work retention. *International Journal of Hospitality Management*, 29 (3): 344–353. doi:10.1016/j.ijhm.2009.08.008.

Panaccio, A., & Vandenberghe, C. 2012. Five-factor model of personality and organizational commitment: The mediating role of positive and negative affective states. *Journal of Vocational Behavior*, 80: 647–658. doi:10.1016/j.jvb.2012.03.002.

Palmer, Daniel E. 2009. Business leadership: Three levels of ethical analysis. *Journal of Business Ethics*, 88, no. 3 (09, 2009): 525–36, https://search.proquest.com/docview/198223433?accountid=10504.

Patockova, L. 2012. Fluctuation and knowledge management in nonprofit organizations. *Procedia – Social and Behavioral Sciences*, 62: 1051–1055. doi:10.1016/j.sbspro.2012.09.179.

Popper, M., & Lipshitz, R. 1993. Putting leadership theory to work: A conceptual framework for theory-based leadership development. *Leadership & Organization Development Journal*, 14 (7): 23. Retrieved from https://search.proquest.com/docview/226910834?accountid=10504

Proudfoot, J. G., Corr, P. J., Guest, D. E., & Dunn, G. 2009. Cognitive-behavioral training to change attributional style improves employee well-being, job satisfaction, productivity, and turnover. *Personality and Individual Differences*, 46: 147–153. doi:10.1016./j/paid.2008.09.018.

Rego, A., Riberio, N., Pina e Cunha, M., & Jesuino, J. C. 2011. How happiness mediates the organizational virtuousness and affective commitment relationship. *Journal of Business Research*, 64: 524–532. doi:10.1016/j.jbusres.2010.04.009.

Rofcanin, Y., & Mehtap, O. 2010. Implications of Leader-Member Exchange Relationship (LMX) Theory and transformational leadership dimensions on subordinate citizenship behavior: An empirical paper from Turkey with services industry focus. *International Journal of Global Business,* 3: 83–101. Retrieved from http:// web.ebscohost.com.ezp.waldenulibrary.org/ehost/detail?vid=7&sid=efac9fc2 -c449-446f-b933-ee29c1232ad9%40sessionmgr112&hid=124&bdata =JnNjb3BlPXNpdGU%3d#db=bth&AN=60870812.

Saradhi,V.V., & Palshikar, G. K. 2011. Employee churn prediction. *Expert Systems with Applications,* 38, 1999–2006. doi:10.1016/j eswa.2010.07.134.

Sorell,T., Guelke,J. & Hadjimatheou, K. 2017. *Security ethics.* New York, NY: Routledge.

Toor, S., & Ofori, G. 2009. Ethical leadership: Examining the relationships with full range leadership model, employee outcomes, and organizational culture. *Journal of Business Ethics,* 90 (4): 533–547. http://dx.doi.org/10.1007/s10551-009-0059-3.

Valcour, M., Ollier-Malaterre,A., Matz-Costa, C., Pitt-Catsouphes, M., & Brown, M. 2011. Influences on employee perceptions of organizational work-life support: Signals and resources. *Journal of Vocational Behavior,* 79 (2): 588. Retrieved from https://search.proquest.com/docview/889261513?accountid=10504.

Walumbwa, F. O.,Wu, C., & Orwa, B. 2008. Contingent reward transactional leadership, work attitudes, and organization citizenship behavior:The role of procedure justice climate perceptions and strength. *The Leadership Quarterly,* 19: 251–265. doi:10.1016/j.leaqua.2008.03.004.

Williams. S. E., Nichols, Q. I., Kirk,A., & Wilson,T. 2010.A recent look at the factors influencing workforce retention in public child welfare. *Children andYouth Review,* 33 (1): 157–160. doi:10.1016/j.childyouth.2010.08.028.

Yasir, M., & Mohamad, N.A. 2016. Ethics and morality: Comparing ethical leadership with servant, authentic and transformational leadership styles. *International Review of Management and Marketing,* 6 (4). Retrieved from https://search.proquest.com/ docview/1796229933?accountid=10504.

Young, A. 2013. Too much information: Ineffective intelligence collection. *Harvard International Review,* 35: 24–27. Retrieved from http://web.ebscohost.com. ezp.waldenulibrary.org/ehost/detail?vid=7&sid=6c62779b-500a-4ab3-b4d6 -3ee728b9f746%40sessionmgr112&hid=124&bdata=JnNjb3BlPXNpdGU %3d#db=bth&AN=87979388.

Zegart, A. B. 2012. The Cuban missile crisis as intelligence failure. *Policy Review,* 175: 23–29. Retrieved from http://web.ebscohost.com.ezp.waldenulibrary.org/ ehost/detail?vid=11&sid=efac9fc2-c449-446f-b933-ee29c1232ad9%40session mgr112&hid=124&bdata=JnNjb3BlPXNpdGU%3d#db=bth&AN=82556887.

Student Reflections on Leadership

Crystal An, J. Lucas Hii, and Yash Kumar
Global Ethical Leaders Society,
Case Western Reserve University

Using a rigorous internal application process, selected members of the Inamori-based student group, Global Ethical Leaders Society (GELS) attended the U.S. Naval Academy Leadership Conference in January 2018, "Breaking Barriers: Obstacles Are Opportunities." The selected three exemplary students have dedicated interests in military ethics and leadership, ethical development, and character building, and they brought valued insight to the discussions with the other participants. Their reflections on ethical leadership in their role as student leaders is especially pertinent to their decision making both on and off campus.

Reflections on NALC 2018
Crystal An

"Glad to be here."

The theme for this year's conference was breaking barriers, and it was clear after listening to such a diverse range of speakers that there are many different ways to overcome obstacles. The one thing that resounded through each keynote, interview, and panel, however, was the manner with which leaders approach their obstacles. Successful leadership in the face of challenges starts with a perspective of gratitude. A sense of gladness to be standing in front of this barrier with an understanding that excellent leadership can only exist in this moment when one is standing face-to-face against an obstacle. Barriers exist solely to define the difference between where we are and where we want to be. Former Blue Angel John Foley gave this state another name in his opening address: the high performance zone.

"It's not dangerous. It's inherently unforgiving."

Another quote from the opening keynote. Foley was referring to flying fighter jets at sonic speeds within eighteen inches of each other, but this mindset is clearly applicable to other challenges that the rest of us are more likely to face in daily life. There is a nuanced but significant difference between feeling fear and being scared. Fear implies a feeling of "stuckness," while being scared stems from one's intuition and keeps us from falling into complacency. Stress and fear will naturally manifest if one views a challenge as dangerous. Thus, leaders must instead view high-stakes situations as merely an environment with less room for error and a greater need for precision.

"You don't have to be perfect to step in the ring."

Society has a tendency to hold girls to a standard of perfection that is unattainable and harmful. A lot of attention has been dedicated to fixing this issue as it pertains to body image, but the expectation of perfection has even more pervasive effects that extend beyond that. Michele Flournoy described a study that showed, when given a list of qualifications required for a job, men are more likely to apply even if they only meet six out of ten requirements as compared to women, who tend to not even apply if they don't meet all ten requirements. Flournoy stressed the importance of teaching women to be brave instead of perfect. The system cannot be fixed until more women build up the courage to enter the ring, and this cannot happen until we make conscientious moves to shatter the societal misconstruction that perfection is a necessary quality for women. Merit should be treated as the baseline for assessment, and excellent performance should be analyzed with gender-blind judgement only.

"Touching the dragon."

Chief James Hatch was a former Navy Seal who worked closely with K9 units and experienced the loss of many friends, both human and canine. After sustaining a severe injury that left him bedridden in a hospital for weeks, Hatch was left with a large amount of free time to contemplate an unbearable amount of guilt. For him, the challenge was in recovery and the obstacles existed primarily in his own mind. Mental health is an enormous issue that has only recently been receiving more attention, but Hatch's story brought up some jarring questions. How do you approach a barrier with a sense of gladness, when, you are in fact, not glad to be here—not even to be living and breathing? How do you face an obstacle eye-to-eye, when even looking into your own eyes in a reflection feels intolerable? Sometimes, leadership is a lot less glamorous than what we expect it to be. Sometimes, as Captain Hatch revealed, you just have to survive the obstacles. There is a stigma against getting help for mental health issues, but all stigma stems from cowardice, and recovery requires the bravery to touch the dragon. For Hatch, it meant revisiting and reliving his traumatic memories; for the rest of us, it is facing our fears and becoming comfortable with the feeling of being scared. The reasons why we touch the dragon are universal. We do it for the people that have saved us, the people that we love, and for the people that we can possibly save in the future. Obstacles were never meant to be easy, but touching the dragon certainly creates a powerful sense of purpose.

"Glad to be here."

From the start to the end of the three days we spent in Annapolis, these opening words ran through my thoughts almost constantly. Glad to have been given the opportunity to be at the US Naval Academy. Glad to be here sitting amongst midshipmen who will one day be integral leaders in our country's military. Glad to be here listening to Under Secretary Michele Flournoy advocating for more young women to step into the ring. Glad to be here shaking the hand of the Red Cross Senior Vice President of Humanitarian Services. Glad that she didn't care how sweaty my palms were. Glad to be here with a Navy Seal sharing his story and baring his soul to educate tomorrow's leaders. Glad to be here, but even more glad to be able to bring some incredible lessons about leadership and obstacles back to Cleveland.

NALC 2018 Recap: Promoting Ethical Leadership with Realistic Optimism
J. Lucas Hii

Defining leadership qualities entails a unique problem where every expression can resonate as cliché and unauthentic. We hear that true leaders inspire action within others and appeal to an embryonic sense of passion that people thrive on. However, during my experience at the NALC 2018, I discovered a less portrayed branch of leadership more accessible to the common person than the heroic figures we idolize and fail to truly understand. Rather than regurgitate the details that shape the ideal leader, I will reflect upon my time at the NALC 2018 to indicate how every individual can embody the spirit of a humble leader focused on daily action. I heard from leaders, despite diverse and controversial pasts, who transformed their character to embody the qualities of an optimistic realist. They all expressed the importance of maintaining optimism during adversity; while prioritizing decision making and risk assessment that is grounded by a realistic perspective. One of the most impactful experiences was hearing Former U.S Secretary of State and U.S Ambassador to the UN, the Honorable Madeleine Albright, speak of her experience during the Rwandan and Darfur genocides. Specifically, the difficulty in proper decision making with limited and sometimes dubious information. Alongside Madeleine Albright, both the Honorable Richard Cheney and General James Conway expressed how a leader must establish credibility through their values and create a culture of authenticity. This authenticity enhances decision making through disagreements and promotes accountability when failures occur. This panel focused on the holistic development of a leader that endures stressful circumstances while remaining composed enough to lead with credibility.

Following the Forrestal Panel, Special Operations Chief Daniel Luna spoke the next morning reinforcing the importance of grit, resilience, and a support system. He stressed more than anything the support system he leaned on to endure terrible circumstances including the loss of many friends and his personal battle with depression. Chief Luna exposed his heart and wore his emotions with authenticity during the address which emphasized his message even more powerfully. Leaders can attempt to remain upbeat and positive on the surface, but a truly powerful leader understands that reality sometimes crushes your soul and all you can do is try to make it through another day. This true demonstration of character encourages reciprocal support when reality is too difficult to handle. Chief Luna highlighted the importance of Faith, Focus, Friends, and Family in order to simply make it through another day. This leadership style is founded in the belief that to lead you first must follow, and that the strongest leader adopts a mentor–mentor relationship never rising above those they lead. They always respect the individuals they take responsibility for, and most of all expose their authentic self in order to make it through the hard days.

I would like to thank GELS and the Inamori Center for Ethics and Excellence for the opportunity to participate in the NALC 2018 which was a privilege that will not be forgotten.

A Leader's Journey to Immortality
Yash Kumar

"The Rainbow Unicorns?"

"Be serious."

"Airbenders?"

"No."

"Callahan Killers?"

"Not bad."

"What about Hornets?"

"Everyone agree?"

After across-the-board nodding, I register our school's nickname as our team name in Tulsa Ultimate Federation's (TUF) high school league. The last three years of my high school experience were a long journey. As I reflect on my experience of creating my school's ultimate team, I truly understand the value of the lessons I learned at USNA 2018.

We have a critical choice. It governs our life philosophy, and how we go about our decision-making process. We must choose between an infinite and finite life.

An infinite life may seem absurd. Isn't all life finite? This was precisely my thought as Simon Sinek gave his talk on the difference between infinite and finite battles. However, I slowly realized that infinite and finite aspects to life do exist. Infinite life exists when people talk about you in the future because your contributions to organizations outlive you. However, finite elements of life only regard power and money, so when you die, you become forgotten.

If I learned anything at USNA, it is that existence is a privilege! What are you doing with this privilege?

Indeed, one must find something fulfilling in order to pursue his/her infinite life. This is an arduous process, one that I continue to struggle with. However, if we abandon this journey, we risk our potential to induce change. While choosing to maximize the finite elements of life is not a wrong choice, I hope you do not live solely by the philosophy of one of my favorite satirical Bollywood movies "Life is a race. If you don't run fast. You will be like a broken anda (egg)."

If you have chosen an infinite journey, then your priority is to find a just cause, a why, something that gives you the willingness to sacrifice and the motivation to do the right thing. With a purpose in hand, a leader must continue to establish a proper culture. The need to do the little things right must be the bedrock. In fact, in crisis, you cannot surge trust. Instead, you must build it gradually. The only way to build trust is to have real relationships, where you know what matters to your team and what is happening in their lives. Through this manner, you are prepared for a crisis. In reality, we do not rise to the occasion, but instead we sink to our training, and for this reason, culture is essential.

Additionally, gratitude must be a staple part of the culture. For success, we need optimism. However, gratitude is often the hardest part for people, including me. This is because the innate human psyche complains, and with a collection of people, complaining exacerbates. However, we must eliminate the "this sucks" lexicon. If my teammates did not care enough to do drills in practice, then why where they there? They had to understand that their dedication to the team and their love for the game drove them to show up for 8 a.m. Saturday practice; they needed to learn to be excited about improving. Thus, with purpose and meaning, people will learn to be grateful in a reinforcing and supportive culture.

Finally, leaders have an additional burden. They must accept situations and take responsibility. You have to be courageous and be responsible for your own morale. Leaders cannot afford to show weakness to the team. Instead, you must show your team that regardless, you will not let them down in any situation. As Churchill once said, "If you're going through hell, keep going."

Overall, I learned that leadership has no relation to a title or authority, as an individual cannot bring team success. Instead, it is about identifying a need and empowering people to maximize their efforts in achieving that shared vision. Through remaining accountable and building a supportive and grateful culture, you can progress towards "immortality" and act in a way that drives the team to pursue the fulfilling purpose.

Talking Foreign Policy Transcript

Talking Foreign Policy is a one-hour radio program, hosted by Case Western Reserve University School of Law Co-Dean Michael Scharf, in which experts discuss the salient foreign policy issues of the day. The quarterly broadcast is produced in partnership between Case Western Reserve University, the only U.S. law school with its own foreign policy talk radio program, and WCPN 90.3 FM ideastream, Cleveland's National Public Radio affiliate. The broadcast on October 5, 2017, addressed the international human rights case Jesner v. Arab Bank. Archived broadcasts are available for viewing in video format online at law.case.edu/TalkingForeignPolicy.

Talking Foreign Policy, October 5, 2017, broadcast[1]

Participants:

Judge Thomas Buergenthal, the youngest survivor of the Auschwitz death camp, who went on to become the Dean of American University Law School, to serve for twelve years as a judge on the Inter-American Court of Human Rights, and then another ten years as the U.S. Judge on the World Court;

Carsten Stahn, one of the foremost experts on the International Criminal Court and the Program Director of the Grotius Centre (The Hague) as well as a professor at Leiden University in The Netherlands;

Milena Sterio, Associate Dean and Professor of Law at Cleveland-Marshall College of Law. Sterio is also one of six permanent editors of the IntLawGrrls blog and an expert in the field of international law;

Avidan Cover, Director of the Institute for Global Law & Policy at Case Western Reserve University School of Law and an expert in national security law. Cover has also litigated national security cases in federal and state courts;

Timothy Webster, Associate Professor of Law, Director of Asian Legal Studies and U.S. Director, Joint Program in International Commercial Law and Dispute Resolution at Case Western Reserve University School of Law;

---

1. Transcribed and annotated by Chelsea Fletcher, Amy Kochert, and Vito Giannola.

SCHARF: You probably remember the tragic story of the 1984 Bhopal disaster, where negligence at Union Carbide Corporation's pesticide plant in India resulted in the release of toxic gas that severely injured or killed over 200,000 local residents.[2] Unfortunately, Bhopal is not an isolated case. It is in this context that Fatou Bensouda, the Chief Prosecutor of the International Criminal Court, recently announced that investigating corporations will be a priority for her office.[3] And on October 14, the U.S. Supreme Court is set to hear the case of *Jesner v. Arab Bank*,[4] a case that will determine if corporations can be sued in U.S. court for the human rights abuses that they commit abroad.

For this broadcast of *Talking Foreign Policy*, we've assembled a panel of human rights experts, including Tom Buergenthal, a judge of the International Court of Justice, who will discuss the cutting-edge issue of corporations on trial, right after the news.

Welcome to *Talking Foreign Policy*. I'm your host Michael Scharf, the Dean of Case Western Reserve University School of Law. In this broadcast, our expert panelists will be discussing corporate liability for human rights abuses. For our program today, we've assembled a panel of leading human rights experts from the United States and Europe.

We'll begin with a one-on-one conversation with Tom Buergenthal, the youngest survivor of the Auschwitz death camp, who went on to become the Dean of American University Law School, to serve for twelve years as a judge on the Inter-American Court of Human Rights, and then another ten years as the U.S. judge on the World Court. Thanks, Judge, for being with us today.

BUERGENTHAL: It's a great pleasure.

SCHARF: So let's start. In 2007, you published *A Lucky Child*,[5] a memoir of surviving Auschwitz as a young boy. How did that experience shape the rest of your life and especially your work in the human rights field?

---

2. See Stuart Diamond, "The Bhopal Disaster: How it Happened," *N.Y. Times* (Jan. 28, 1985), http://www.nytimes.com/1985/01/28/world/the-bhopal-disaster-how-it-happened.html?pagewanted=all.

3. See International Criminal Court, Office of the Prosecutor, Policy Paper on Case Selection and Prioritisation, ¶ 41, (Sep. 15, 2016), https://www.icc-cpi.int/itemsDocuments/20160915_OTP-Policy_Case-Selection_Eng.pdf, (giving special consideration to crimes involving destruction of the environment, the illegal exploitation of natural resources or the illegal dispossession of land).

4. Jesner v. Arab Bank, PLC, 137 S. Ct. 1432 (2017).

5. Thomas Buergenthal, *A Lucky Child* (2010).

BUERGENTHAL: Well, I suppose I would not have written about human rights if I had not been in the camps. It also shaped me in terms of a need to write about it, and to contribute in one way or another to a situation where we can prevent the things that happened to me and that are still happening to a lot of people in the world.

SCHARF: You were just mentioning before we came on the show that you are currently working on a report about the North Korean concentration camps, and I hadn't heard anything about that. Do you want to tell us a little bit about that project?

BUERGENTHAL: Well, it's a project about, as you mentioned, about the work camps, what they call work camps, but in fact, they are worse than concentration camps. I thought I knew everything about concentration camps and how bad things can be in it. I must say, what I heard, if it is true—and I have no reason to assume that it's not true—this is much worse than anything I've experienced in the camp.

SCHARF: That's hard to believe because many people know about what you went through in Auschwitz, and North Korea is worse.

BUERGENTHAL: Now this is, for example, something. They would arrest one person and then, because he was guilty of something that they say he was guilty of, they would take the entire family with him. They had methods of cruelty in terms of getting rid of babies [of women] that were impregnated by the guards. Methods that, I must say, I'd never heard of, what you can do, when it would be just as easy to kill the baby. Just the utter cruelty and inhuman cruelty that, to me, was something I'd never heard of. So if all of this is true, it is the worst, I think, that the world has ever heard of, what's happening in these camps.[6]

SCHARF: And this is from somebody who not only lived through that, but you were a judge in so many human rights cases, and also human rights cases that came before the World Court. Let me ask you about one of the cases you presided over when you were at the Inter-American Court of Human Rights, which you ended up being the president of. This was the case about whether the Honduran government had to pay compensation to families of victims of forced disappearances that had occurred during the

---

6. See generally U.S. Dep't of State, Bureau of Democracy, H.R. and Lab., Democratic People's Republic of Korea 2016 Human Rights Report 3 (2016).

1980s.[7] Many people say that was the most important of the Inter-American Court's cases. What was the significance of that precedent?

BUERGENTHAL: Well for one thing, it was really the first really important case to reach us. And secondly, there had been no decisions in international courts about international law and disappearances. So we really had to deal with the subject and come up with a theory in which we could deal with these terrible, again, cruelties.

SCHARF: And part of that case was that the government was responsible for prosecuting the people, and they couldn't give amnesty to the individuals who were involved, right? So if the U.S.—

BUERGENTHAL: Let me just interrupt you, because what was interesting particularly in this case was that the government would say, "Well, this person hasn't disappeared if he went to see his girlfriend." But the problem was, how do we prove that somebody, that the government, is responsible for a disappearance, when everything was done to keep it secret? And so, to develop the theory in these cases, we've set precedents for many others that are now happening in many parts of the world.

SCHARF: But the idea that governments are, after these things come to light, responsible for making sure that there are remedies to the individuals, is one of the biggest things that came out of that line of cases. If the U.S. Supreme Court decides that corporations cannot be sued for human rights abuses that they commit abroad, would that violate the spirit of the line of cases we were discussing?

BUERGENTHAL: Very much so. I mean the whole idea that corporations somehow are exempt or immune, and can only be tried in their own countries, and [under] certain circumstances, and even not that—that's not international law.

SCHARF: So then let's take your career forward to the International Court of Justice where you served for ten years. This is the court that is in The Hague. It's known as the World Court. It's the court that hears cases between countries. While you were there, it's pretty rare, I think, that a judge of that Court will side against his own country. And there were several cases involving the United States that you sat on, and in two of those cases, you did decide that the U.S. was wrong.[8] These are the cases that

---

7. Velásquez–Rodríguez v. Honduras, 28 I.L.M. 291 (July 29, 1988).
8. LaGrand (Ger. v. U.S.), Judgment, 2001 I.C.J. Rep. 466 (June 27); Avena and Other

you held that the United States failed to advise foreigners of their consular rights in proceedings that resulted in death sentences, and that that was a violation of international law. Did you feel at the time that it was risky to exercise that kind of independence to go against your own government?

BUERGENTHAL: No, and I should tell you that this question was asked even by my colleagues. And my reply was always, "I'm sure I'm not going to end up in Siberia for proceeding the way I proceeded." It seemed to me, first of all, the U.S. put me there because they had confidence in me. And that meant that they also had to take my interpretations, the way I felt it should be interpreted.

SCHARF: But that's rare, and in other countries, many times, the individual judges don't feel that kind of security.

BUERGENTHAL: I suppose, but, I must say, it was easy for me. Because, and I should tell you that nobody ever from the U.S. government even mentioned it to me, which is interesting. So no, I'm not a hero in that regard. I just felt I was free. And also, it was important that somebody set the precedent that you can do that.

SCHARF: Well, you were a little bit heroic in the eyes of many who followed your career. Not only by standing up to the U.S. government from time to time as a judge, but also, you weren't very shy about dissenting from the majority of other judges, and especially in cases involving human rights, which is really your bailiwick, your expertise. So I'm thinking about the Belgium arrest warrants case.[9] There, the majority held that the foreign minister of the Congo was immune from suit for crimes against humanity. Why do you believe that that was the wrong decision?

BUERGENTHAL: Well, because I think they were applying international law that maybe was valid twenty, thirty years before the case was decided, but international law had changed. At that point, we already looked at the Rome Statute, or the drafts of the Rome Statute, and people holding these positions were not immune anymore. So it seemed to me that it was a new world, new international law, new international law that was needed. And if anybody can make those pronouncements, it's the International Court of Justice, and it should have done it. I was fortunate to be accompanied by two people whom I regard as great international lawyers, so it was easy.

Mexican Nationals (Mex. v. U.S.), Judgment, 2004 I.C.J. Rep. 12 (Mar. 31).
9. Arrest Warrant of 11 April 2000 (Dem. Rep. Congo v. Belg.), Judgment, 2002 I.C.J. Rep. 3 (Feb. 14).

SCHARF: Now, unfortunately, they didn't follow your advice on that, and I think that that did set back international law. I noticed that in Africa there is a new court of Africa criminal law being set up, and it will exempt the heads of state from responsibility.[10] And so, it seems like that, you know, sometimes a case like that can propel international law forward or set it back.

BUERGENTHAL: I shouldn't be saying that about the International Court. But I think the problem at that time, in the International Court of Justice, was that too many former diplomats sat on the court.

SCHARF: Instead of career judges?

BUERGENTHAL: Career judges, or academics, or human rights specialists—and that has an impact. And of course, they should be there, but it's very difficult to change their minds.

SCHARF: You know, even career judges can be political, and I think we see that especially at our Supreme Court. Later in the program, we're going to be discussing the U.S. Supreme Court's case of *Jesner v. Arab Bank*, which will decide whether corporations can be sued for human rights violations. If you, who are nonpolitical and have had such a career in the human rights world, were sitting on that bench, how would you decide the case?

BUERGENTHAL: Oh, I would hold that corporations, like individuals, can be tried for violations of international law, particularly serious violations of international law.

SCHARF: And you think that's an easy case?

BUERGENTHAL: Well, it's not easy because two lower courts—well, one lower court—held the other way.

SCHARF: I mean they basically said that international law only applies to states, not corporations. Do you think that's right?

BUERGENTHAL: I mean that's another notion. That in the 21st century, to say that in itself, shows a misunderstanding of what contemporary international law is all about.

SCHARF: You know, even back after World War II, for the kinds of atrocities that were committed to you and the many people who didn't survive

---

10. See Protocol on Amendments to the Protocol on the Statute of the African Court of Justice and Human Rights, art. 46A bis (June 27, 2014), https://au.int/en/treaties/protocol-amendments-protocol-statute-african-court-justice-and-human-rights.

Auschwitz, they did prosecute the Krupp Corporation leaders for that.[11] And so, it's not like there's not precedent for going after corporations. It's not like corporations haven't been involved in atrocities. So, you're now working on a sequel to your book. Can you tell us a little bit about that?

BUERGENTHAL: Well it's—I call it preliminarily *My Second Life*. I was told by a number of publishers in Europe that they heard from their readers who said "Well, your *Lucky Child* book, your first book, you stopped writing it when you arrived in the U.S. at the age of seventeen, and what happened to him afterwards?" And, particularly in Europe, they wanted to know what happened to this kid after all those years. And so, they asked me whether I would be interested in doing it and, of course, I couldn't resist. And it's not as easy to write, because the first book was easy to write, it just flowed out of me. First of all, I've gotten a little more mature about what I can say and what I cannot say. But it's just much harder and, of course, all these years I've spent in the U.S. But I'm writing it in a way as dealing with episodes of my life, because I've come to the conclusion that if I began at the beginning of, say, when I arrived in New York, I would have to have about at least a hundred twenty years of my life.

SCHARF: It'd be like Winston Churchill's many volumes. We only have a couple of seconds left before our station break, but can you tell us what you think the theme of your life has been?

BUERGENTHAL: Well, the title of my first book was *A Lucky Child*, and I'm often asked by people who say that luck is not really the way to deal with it. It was luck. Because if people speak of divine intervention and things like this, that would be such an arrogant notion. And I felt I survived out of luck because so many—a million and a half Jewish children—did not survive. So that's the theme, and the theme is to prevent that from happening to other children.

SCHARF: Judge Buergenthal, I think all of us who have had the privilege of knowing you feel that we are the lucky ones, and that you have given so much to the world of human rights law. It's time for a short station break. When we return, we will dive more deeply into the case of *Jesner v. Arab Bank* with our panel of experts. We'll be back in just a moment.

Welcome back to *Talking Foreign Policy* brought to you by Case Western Reserve University and WCPN 90.3 ideastream. I'm Michael Scharf, the

---

11. U.S. v. Krupp, Trial 10 U.S. Military Tribunal III (1948).

Dean of Case Western Reserve University School of Law. We're talking today about whether corporations should be liable for human rights abuses committed abroad. In this segment we're going to bring some local human rights experts into conversation. We're being joined today by Milena Sterio, the Associate Dean of Cleveland Marshall College of Law, who is a regular guest on our show. It's great to have you back.

STERIO: It's a pleasure to be here.

SCHARF: We also have with us Case Western Reserve Law Professor Avidan Cover, who is director of the school's Institute for Global Security Law and Policy and runs the school's human rights clinic.

COVER: It's great to be here.

SCHARF: Avidan is sitting where Judge Buergenthal was just. We are also joined by Case Western Reserve Professor Tim Webster, who teaches human rights law and has published cutting-edge research in this area.

WEBSTER: Thank you, Michael.

SCHARF: Finally, we have Carsten Stahn, who is our special guest from Europe. He is an expert in international criminal law. He's the Director of the Grotious Center and a professor at Leiden University. Carsten, thanks for coming all the way in from The Hague.

STAHN: Thank you. Wonderful to be here Michael.

SCHARF: I understand there's a big human rights case about to be argued at the U.S. Supreme Court. Let's start with some background. Milena, can you start by telling us what this case is all about?

STERIO: Sure, the case is called *Jesner versus Arab Bank*. The plaintiffs are a group of victims of terrorist attacks that took place between 1995 and 2005 in Israel, the West Bank, and Gaza.[12] The defendant, the Arab Bank, is a bank located in Jordan which has over five hundred branches throughout the world.[13] The plaintiffs alleged that the bank supported terrorism by maintaining accounts for known terrorists, by accepting donations that the bank knew would be used to fund terrorism, and by distributing millions of dollars of payments to families of suicide bombers.[14] Now the bank

---

12. *In re* Arab Bank, PLC Alien Tort Statute Litigation, 808 F.3d 144, 149 (2d Cir. 2015).
13. *Id.*; Arab Bank: Global Network, Arab Bank, http://www.arabbank.com/en/globalnetwork.aspx.
14. *In re* Arab Bank, PLC Alien Tort Statute Litigation, 808 F.3d at 149.

says none of this is true. It says basically, "I'm a bank, I'm a normal bank. I don't engage in or I don't support terrorism." And the bank describes itself as an active and leading partner in the socio-economic development in the Middle East.[15]

SCHARF: So the victims are from what country?

STERIO: The victims are mostly from Israel and from the Middle East.

SCHARF: And the bank is from what country?

STERIO: The bank is based in Jordan, although it has branches around the world.

SCHARF: This case isn't before an international court, it's right here in the United States. What is it about U.S. law that allows foreigners to sue other foreigners for human rights violations in U.S. quarter?

STERIO: The plaintiffs are actually using a U.S. federal statute called the Alien Tort Claims Act (ATCA).[16] The Alien Tort Claims Act is a federal law that gives U.S. federal courts jurisdiction over civil actions by aliens for torts committed in violation of the law of nations or a treaty of the United States.[17] And so here we have plaintiffs who are aliens, foreign citizens, who are suing another alien, a bank located in Jordan, for a tort committed in violation of international law which would be support of terrorism.

SCHARF: Well this seems like a very modern statute. When was it adopted?

STERIO: The statute was adopted back in 1789 and was part of the original Judiciary Act,[18] which essentially set up our federal courts. It basically sat dormant until 1980—so for almost 200 years nobody had ever used it. Then in 1980 arose this case called *Filartiga*,[19] where two plaintiffs from Paraguay decided to resurrect this federal statute and use it to bring a lawsuit against another Paraguayan citizen for torture. In that case the United States Appellate Court, the Second Circuit, held that the Alien Tort Statute could be used for this kind of a lawsuit by a foreign plaintiff, an alien, if the tort is a violation of international law.[20]

---

15. Chairman's Message, Arab Bank, http://www.arabbank.com/en/messagefromchairman.aspx.

16. 28 U.S.C. § 1350 (2012).

17. *Id.*

18. *Id.*

19. Filartiga v. Pena-Irala, 630 F.2d 876 (2d Cir. 1980).

20. *Id.*

SCHARF: Now Tim Webster, you teach human rights law; you teach the Alien Tort Claims Act litigation area. It doesn't seem like the U.S. Supreme Court likes this Alien Tort Claims Act very much. In two recent decisions the *Sosa*[21] case and in the *Kiobel*[22] case the Supreme Court has greatly cut back on the usefulness of this statute. Can you tell us about those cases?

WEBSTER: Sure, yeah. So there's two cases, and again our Supreme Court is there to help clarify what federal statutes mean and what they can do. The first case is from 2004, it's called *Sosa*. The second case is a more recent one called *Kiobel* from 2013. Let me go back to *Sosa* for a minute. What *Sosa* did—and this gets to what Professor Milena was just talking about—*Sosa* says that this law, this Alien Tort Claims Act, is jurisdictional.[23] What that means for people who are not lawyers is that this opens up U.S. federal courts to lawsuits from anywhere around the world. It doesn't talk about the cause of action. It doesn't tell us what the remedy is. It says only that U.S. federal courts can hear these kinds of actions. The second piece of *Sosa* suggests that the kinds of actions—the kinds of torts that are permissible in the United States have to be very specific.[24] They say if we go back and look at the 1789 law, there needs to be a high degree of specificity. And the Supreme Court said in 2004 that it has to be something along the lines of piracy or torture.[25] Torture wasn't one they actually mentioned, but they said these need to be very specific norms we're talking about, we're not letting everybody in here. These norms have to have been articulated clearly and specifically in order for our federal courts to be open for these foreign plaintiffs. So that's the *Sosa* decision. But again, you can see by requiring this specificity, how other kinds of acts would be excluded.

SCHARF: So human rights violations that are short of torture or even terrorism—it's not clear that the Court would think there's a universal definition of terrorism or for piracy?

WEBSTER: Absolutely, yeah. The Supreme Court said the norms that we're going to allow these cases to proceed under have to be very specific, clearly defined, and there has to be a widely accepted definition.

SCHARF: Okay then, what about the *Kiobel* case?

---

21. Sosa v. Alvarez-Machain, 542 U.S. 692 (2004).
22. Kiobel v. Royal Dutch Petroleum Co., 569 U.S. 108 (2013).
23. *Sosa*, 542 U.S. at 714.
24. *Id*. at 725.
25. *Id*. at 724–25.

WEBSTER: *Kiobel* comes around you know nine years later—and you set this up quite nicely with Professor Sterio—you said look here we in the *Jesner* case we have a foreign plaintiff suing a foreign defendant for actions that took place abroad. The concern here is why are we here in the United States? Why are we having these lawsuits where there's very little discernible U.S. interest at all? The Supreme Court in *Kiobel* said we are going to place a presumption against extraterritoriality application.[26] That's a mouthful. What that means is: what is the United States' interest in having our courts hear this case? The language there said there is a presumption that we should not hear these cases, but that presumption can be overcome. We will allow these cases if the plaintiff can show that the action somehow "touches and concerns."[27] That's the magical language. Does this case touch and concern the United States? Now what does "touch and concern" mean? No one is exactly sure, it's somewhat vague language. In one of the concurring opinions offered by Justice Breyer, he said touching concern means the following: (a) it means the conduct took place on U.S. soil; (b) it means the defendant is an American; or (c) this is the arguably the catch-all: the defendants' conduct affects an important national interest of the United States.[28] So the first two are quite clear, quite specific. The third one says: "Does this affect an important national interest of the United States?" You could argue that preventing terrorism or preventing the financing of terrorism, which is what *Jesner* is about, represents an important U.S. national interest. But that's the hurdle, that is the obstacle that *Jesner* needs to surmount in order to continue.

SCHARF: The Arab Bank in this case also has branch offices in New York and does business in the United States. Maybe some of the counter the terrorist financing in this case went through U.S. banks.

WEBSTER: Absolutely, yes. If we can show that, then it would touch and concern the United States.

SCHARF: Right. So the issue that the Supreme Court wanted to use this case for is based on the defendant's argument that corporations cannot be liable under the Alien Tort Claims Act because only governments can violate international law. Milena Sterio told us that the statute only allows the courts to prosecute suits for violations of international law. Judge

---

26. *Kiobel*, 569 U.S. at 117.
27. *Id*. at 124–25.
28. *Id*. at 127 (Breyer, J., concurring).

Buergenthal, who was here in our earlier segment, he said that's old think. What do you think? Is there anything to this argument?

WEBSTER: To take that argument on frontally, you and I were talking about piracy, and even in 1789 piracy was a violation of international law. Now piracy back then and even now is generally not committed by governments, right? It's human beings and arguably even groups of human beings, arguably even corporations, that participate in piracy. There are opinions from the 1790s, there were opinions from the early 20th century that say particularly with regard to the Alien Tort Claims Act—that the attorney general of the United States penned—that said corporations can be liable.[29] Even though we haven't seen a lot of cases, and of course there are Alien Tort Claims Act that have held corporations can be liable—this idea that corporations can't be liable, only governments can be liable for international law, has been if not debunked at least challenged for a couple of centuries now.

SCHARF: We'll see where the Supreme Court goes on this one. Professor Avidan Cover, you teach human rights clinic, you litigate these kinds of cases, you're a national security law expert. From a human rights perspective, what do you think is at stake in this case? Big picture, what's this precedent likely to do?

COVER: To use a certain international leader's terminology, this is a huge case. I think what's at stake for human rights is that the United States is in step with the developing trends in the world on human rights. There's a general growing recognition that corporations should be held liable for human rights violations. We've seen it a number of the United States allies. The United Kingdom and the Netherlands have recognized corporate liability in their domestic statutes regarding genocide and such other crimes.[30] I think this case is a great support for that. Now it's interesting that the issue the court accepted as it's formally presented is whether corporations are categorically exempt from liability under the Alien Tort Statute (ATS). From that language, a lot of court critics suggest and infer a favorable position in terms of finding there will be at least at some level corporate liability. Just the way that the court phrased the question is limiting and shows that the

---

29. *See* Curtis A. Bradley, *Attorney General Bradford's Opinion and the Alien Tort Statute*, 106 Am. J. Int'l L. 509 (2012) (suggesting that the 1795 opinion supported some extraterritorial application of the ATS).

30. See SR Art. 51, lid 2, (Neth.) (applying the act to all "persons"); Interpretation Act 1978 c. 30, § 5, sch. I (U.K.) (stating that the word "'person' includes a body of persons corporate or unincorporated").

court is not going to buy into that kind of prohibition. But it's interesting what Tim was focusing on in that second issue; one question is whether the court may be able to yet again kick the can down the road and avoid that question by simply finding that the matter is basically extraterritorial, right, and there's no nexus and evade at least for the time being whether indeed corporations can be held liable.

SCHARF: So Professor Webster was saying that there's a national security interest. You're saying there's this huge human rights interest. Against that is the business law interests in the business community, and often courts are very concerned about that. Milena Sterio, the U.S. Chamber of Commerce and other business groups have filed briefs[31] with the defendants—what's their argument?

STERIO: From the business side, from the corporate side, the fact that corporations could potentially be liable for human rights abuses is not a good thing. The U.S. Chamber of Commerce and other business groups have filed briefs with the Supreme Court arguing against extending the Alien Tort Statute to cover corporate liability.[32] Some of the arguments that have been raised in these briefs is that the Alien Tort Statute lawsuits against corporations have run rampant in recent decades. That there have been dozens, if not hundreds of ATS cases against U.S. and foreign corporations that do business in two dozen industry sectors, arising in corporate activity throughout the world. And how holding corporations liable is not a good thing because it will stifle their business activity, it will harm everyone's interested in sense. So they're really squarely against this.

SCHARF: Avidan, did you meet Justice Gorsuch when he came to Case Western a year ago?

COVER: Yes, very briefly.

SCHARF: Okay so the newest justice of the Supreme Court, a conservative justice nominated by Republican President Donald Trump, confirmed by Republican-controlled Senate, is Neil Gorsuch. What do you think his addition to the court is likely to do to the outcome of what might be a very close case?

---

31. Brief for the Chamber of Commerce of the United States of American, the National Foreign Trade Council, USA Engage, the United States Council for International Business, and the American Petroleum Institute as Amici Curiae Supporting Neither Party, Jesner v. Arab Bank, PLC, 137 S. Ct. 1432 (2017) (No. 16-499).
32. *Id.*

COVER: Right, it's very interesting. Justice Gorsuch only joined the court four days, or he was confirmed only a few days after cert was granted in this matter. He didn't play any role in deciding whether to take this case or not. He is a justice who he had been part of the Tenth Circuit *Hobby Lobby* decision, holding that corporations have perhaps certain religious liberty interests.[33] So he may be viewed as someone who is certainly very sympathetic to corporations. Certainly, plenty of his jurisprudence while he was on the Tenth Circuit as an Appellate judge suggests that he would be sympathetic to the corporation's position. That said, he also served in government. And the federal government's position on this, while acknowledging that corporations can be and even should be held liable under the Alien Tort Statute, is of the view that the extraterritoriality decision should be determined first. And that in fact national security implications, of perhaps improvidently deciding this case and affecting the relationship with Jordan in particular, could adversely affect national security concerns. I could certainly see Justice Gorsuch—who holds himself to be a strict constructionist reading the statute as narrowly as possible, reading the courts role as narrowly as possible—might opt for that second route. Which is to say that there is no nexus and so again, to kick that can down the road.

SCHARF: Now for the other justices. They sort of painted themselves into a corner with the *Citizens United* case.[34] *Citizens United*, as the listeners might recall, is this case that President Obama said was the worst decision the Supreme Court ever had.[35] It's the case that said that corporations are people for purposes of the First Amendment and therefore have a right to contribute to political campaigns and cannot be constrained by the federal legislation.[36] So if corporations are people for purposes of giving a lot of money to political campaigns, Milena Sterio or Avidan Cover—why can't they be people for purposes of human rights violations?

STERIO: I actually think that the Supreme Court in this case, in *Jesner*, will actually decide the corporations can be liable. I think it will be a very narrow holding. I think Justice Roberts will write an opinion where he will specify a very narrow set of circumstances under which corporations

---

33. Burwell v. Hobby Lobby Stores, 134 S. Ct. 2751 (2014).
34. Citizens United v. Fed. Election Comm'n, 558 U.S. 310 (2010).
35. *Statement from the President, The White House* (Jan. 21, 2015), https://obamawhitehouse.archives.gov/the-press-office/2015/01/21/statement-president.
36. *Citizens United*, 558 U.S. at 365–66.

can be held liable for human rights violations. I think that would be in line with the *Citizens United* case, because if corporations have free speech rights then certainly they can commit human rights violations. I think it would be very unpopular for the Supreme Court to rule that corporations are categorically exempt from this line of lawsuits.

SCHARF: Carsten Stahn, you've been very patient over there from the Netherlands, and we're going to bring you into the next segment. Are you over in Europe following this case? Is this something that is on the radar of Europeans?

STAHN: The issue is very much on the radar of Europeans. I've seen a couple of cases in Europe where cases have been brought. For instance, there have been some proceedings concerning Mercedes-Benz for its involvement in enforced disappearance during the Argentinian dictatorship.[37] It's an issue which, because of the diversity of different domestic systems, raises a lot of interest.

SCHARF: All right so with the few seconds we have left in this segment, Avidan Cover, how do you think the case is going to be decided?

COVER: I kind of like Milena's take on it. I can't imagine it will be an unequivocal embrace of corporate liability under ATS, but I think they'll try and limit it as much as possible.

SCHARF: So five-four in favor of the plaintiffs?

COVER: Yeah with a certain narrow exception.

SCHARF: Milena?

STERIO: I absolutely agree. The way the Supreme Court has framed the issue is taking the plaintiffs way of framing the issue, which indicates the Supreme Court is more likely to side with the plaintiffs.

SCHARF: Professor Webster, you were saying they might dodge the case all the issue altogether. What do you think?

WEBSTER: I would agree with my co-panelists here, but I would just underline that they will take the narrowest possible ruling that they can.

SCHARF: Which might be to say since the bank isn't an American bank and there's not enough of a connection, that the case will not go forward, right?

---

37. Daimler AG v. Bauman, 134 S. Ct. 746 (2014).

WEBSTER: Possibly, or they can say this does implicate a major national interest of preventing the financing of terrorism, so we do think again, citing Justice Breyer's concurrence that this does affect U.S. national interests in a significant robust manner.

SCHARF: Well everybody out there who's following the Supreme Court this term, hold on to your seat belts cause it's going to be a bumpy ride, and this is just one of the first cases that will be decided. I hope this discussion has shed some light on the importance and likely outcome of the *Jesner v. Arab Bank* case. It's going to be time for another break in just a few seconds. When we return we'll talk about the international effort to criminally prosecute corporations for human rights violations. Back in a moment.

SCHARF: This is Michael Scharf, and we're back with *Talking Foreign Policy*. I'm joined today by some of the world's foremost international law experts. We've been talking about the liability of corporations for human rights abuses. In this final segment, we will look at the International Criminal Court's new focus on prosecuting crimes committed by corporations. In the studio, we have Professor Timothy Webster from Case Western Reserve University School of Law, Associate Dean Milena Sterio from Cleveland Marshall School or Law, Avidan Cover, the Director of the National Security Law Center at Case Western Reserve University, and all the way from The Hague, the Netherlands, we have Carsten Stahn, a professor at Leiden University.

Carsten, you are one of the foremost experts on the International Criminal Court. This is not the World Court that Judge Buergenthal sat on; this is the court that prosecutes individuals for the worst crimes known to humankind. Instead, it lies in The Hague where you're located, and you run, and I assist you with, an International Criminal Court Moot Court Competition where students from all over the world participate and learn about it. So can you give the listeners some background about how the ICC works and what kinds of cases it focuses on?

STAHN: Thank you, Michael. The ICC is the first global court, which tries international crimes like genocide, war crimes, and potentially in the future, aggression. First, its jurisdiction is very limited, so it only tries individuals.[38] That means it doesn't try corporate criminal responsibility

---

38. See *Michael P. Scharf, Results of the Rome Conference for an International Criminal Court*, American Soc'y of Int'l Law (Aug. 11, 1998), https://www.asil.org/insights/volume/3/issue/10/results-rome-conference-international-criminal-court.

as such. Second, the court can only try nationals of state parties or crimes which have been committed on the territory of states parties. A couple of states like the United States, Russia, and China are not a party to the statute, and recently African states like Burundi or South Africa have indicated their intention to even withdraw from the statute, so these are issues that the court has to struggle with.[39] In addition, it's complementary to domestic jurisdiction. That means whenever there is a good domestic case the ICC will not step in. The role of the court in this will remain limited.[40] But the few cases that the ICC does is usually important regarding the impact that they have. It's the message that the court sends that is important.

SCHARF: You said that when they drafted the court statute, they purposely left out liability for juridical persons, which means corporations. Only natural persons who are people can be prosecuted by the court. In your opinion does that create a gap in international criminal law that corporations can exploit?

STAHN: Indeed, it goes back to the famous Nuremberg precedent, which states that crimes are committed by men, not by abstract entities.[41] Since then, France proposed in 1998 that the ICC should have jurisdiction over corporations precisely to increase the rights of victims, including access to compensation through criminal proceedings.[42] This, obviously, didn't get enough consensus because our domestic systems still differ on how to treat corporations.

SCHARF: I was talking briefly with Judge Buergenthal on the first segment about the Krupp Corporation which was prosecuted at Nuremberg. There's an interesting story behind that. Krupp Sr., the real president and head of the corporation, was too ill and frail to be prosecuted. So they grabbed his son Krupp Jr., because he had the same last name. However, he was one of the three that were acquitted at the Nuremberg Trials and the reason for that, what most experts say, is that the father was guilty, not the son. Ultimately, it should have been the corporation that they went

---

39. *See* Abraham Joseph, *Why Did South Africa, Burundi and Gambia Decide to the Leave the International Criminal Court?* The Wire (Jan. 1, 2016) https://thewire.in/76869/why-did-south-africa-burundi-and-gambia-decide-to-leave-the-international-criminal-court/.
40. *Summary of the Key Provisions of the ICC Statute, Human Rights Watch* (Dec. 1, 1998, 3:22 PM), https://www.hrw.org/news/1998/12/01/summary-key-provisions-icc-statute.
41. *Id.*
42. *Id.*

after, but they didn't have jurisdiction.[43] So that's the problem: if a court doesn't get the right defendant, corporations who are made up of a collective of board members and officers, can get away with heinous things. So Carsten, even after the Krupp Corporation case, there has been a lot of cases against corporate officers in international tribunals. I know in the Rwanda tribunal, they went after the president of a tea company that had facilitated genocide using his employees.

Also, the president of a radio program that broadcasted all sorts of incitement to commit genocide. So there's nothing really new about going after corporations, is there?

STAHN: There's a distinction between the extent we can hold corporate agents accountable for what the corporation as such has done. Here we've seen recent developments in the context of both the International Criminal Court, as well as in the African context, to hold to try to bridge the gap and to increase business accountability. The ICC prosecutor [who] wanted to bring cases against corporations at the beginning of the situation in the Democratic Republic of Congo on diamonds is this the obvious example.[44] However, the court has to be very selective in its focus so only recently did the problem gain attention. The ICC prosecutor developed a new policy paper in which they then identified some of the types of violations that the ICC might look into, even if it can't look into the issues of corporate criminal responsibility as such.[45]

SCHARF: So what were those?

STAHN: For instance, illegal exploitation of resources, land grabbing or destruction of the environment. There has been a communication brought against Chevron for instance for intoxicating the environment in Ecuador through its activities.[46] So these are the potential issues that might come before the ICC.

SCHARF: So in those cases, what you think will happen is the ICC will investigate the corporations but ultimately, they won't prosecute the cor-

---

43. U.S. v. Krupp, Trial 10 U.S. Military Tribunal III (1948).

44. International Criminal Court Investigations DRC, Global Policy Forum, https://www.globalpolicy.org/international-justice/the-international-criminal-court/icc-investigations/28595.html.

45. ICC Office of the Prosecutor, Policy Paper on Case Selection and Prioritization, https://www.icc-cpi.int/itemsDocuments/20160915_OTP-Policy_Case-Selection_Eng.pdf.

46. *See* Lachlan Markay, *ICC Won't Prosecute Chevron*, The Wash. Free Beacon (Apr. 2 2015, 3:15 PM), http://freebeacon.com/issues/icc-wont-prosecute-chevron/.

porations as such. They'll go after some officer who they believe is most responsible.

STAHN: Indeed, this is probably what will happen. They will try to trace the patterns of crimes, they might identify some of the violations. Some of the cases might not even go to trial. It might be that the ICC looks into something that it identifies as a violation, which might have a tremendous impact on domestic states action on corporate policies. Of course, if you're in the headlines with the ICC, what you have done is made transparent and can have a grave impact on the corporation.

SCHARF: You know, there are a lot of corporations that were involved in the Nazi Holocaust atrocities that still exist today under different names. However, you can trace their ownership all the way back to the war. Would you say that it's a failure only to prosecute an individual? When you prosecute individuals for individual crimes, you lock them up sometimes for life if it's genocide, and then they can't commit the crimes anymore. But if you only take an officer out of a corporation and the corporation continues to exist, what's the deterrent?

STAHN: Absolutely. I think a fraction of the corporate injustice, and I think the big tragedy is that in most of these cases particularly in inferential environments—if we try individuals, the profit that companies gained from these investments, from the activities—they're not taken into account. That means that victims often miss out on remedies. That's the big tragedy that we face, and this is why some more recent instruments, for instance like the Malabo Protocol established in the African Union, now charge corporate criminal responsibilities precisely to close this gap.[47]

SCHARF: It's not likely that they're going to amend the ICC statute so maybe you can prosecute people in Africa or maybe domestically in Europe or even in the United States. However, in front of the International Criminal Court, a corporation is going to be free and clear, but its officers may not be. Now a prosecutor of the ICC wants to go after the corporations, even if it's only the officers that they can get a hold of. Avidan, Milena, and Tim—do you think that's a good idea? Is the new priority that the prosecutor has announced—going after corporations—the right thing for the International Criminal Court to be focusing on?

47. *Malabo Protocol: Legal and Institutional Implications of The Merged and Expanded African Court, Amnesty International* (Jan. 22, 2016) https://www.amnesty.org/en/documents/afr01/3063/2016/en/.

COVER: I think it's a critical piece of what she should be focusing on. As Carsten identified, we know of issues of minimal mineral extraction and appropriation. These sorts of things are being done at the hands of corporations, and whatever kinds of accountability, retribution or deterrence, can be achieved through those investigations, through the notoriety that is achieved, I think those are a critical piece of our legal system.

STERIO: I think it is important because, as Carsten and Avidan already pointed out—there are cases where going after the corporate officers is really difficult, because if you're trying to impose individual criminal responsibilities on some of the corporate officers, you have to show for example that they had the requisite criminal intent to commit specific acts. That they committed the acts or somehow aided and abetted in the commission of the acts, and that sometimes [is] very difficult to do. So going after the officers is sometimes going to be impossible, despite the fact that corporations might be committing pretty horrific violations of human rights and other crime. So I think this will, you know—going after corporations is important to close that gap.

SCHARF: Tim, do you agree? If you have cases about genocide and cases about corporate damage to the environment, is there equality of those two?

WEBSTER: I'm going to take a slightly different approach than the co-panelists here and again, thinking about the ICC as an institution and as an institution that's trying to make sure that its legitimacy is respected around the world—like Professor Stahn mentioned, a couple of countries in Africa had signaled their intention to withdraw. We know that China, Russia, the United States and numerous other Asian countries have not joined the ICC.[48] So here I would say we need to look at the Rome Statute. We had this conversation back in 1998. The French government said why can't we have criminal corporate liability?[49] The discussion said no, we couldn't have that. I don't fancy myself a strict constructionist, but I think when we have an institution that is fighting for a legitimacy, I think it may overreach to investigate corporate criminal liability when it has not been specifically authorized to take that within its mandate.

SCHARF: You don't agree, Milena?

STERIO: I would just mention this: the U.S. ambassador for war crimes, David Scheffer, who was present at the Rome Statute negotiation, has

---

48. *See* Scharf, *supra* note 51.
49. *Id.*

written and spoken about this, and he says that one of the reasons that this issue of corporate responsibility was dropped and wasn't adopted as part of the Rome Statute was that the consensus at the time was that most national laws at the time did not have provisions for criminal liability for corporations, and that most national laws have evolved since then and now do.[50] So that would be a counter-argument.

WEBSTER: Some countries have now imposed corporate criminal liability.[51] I believe the minority. So if we can say a hundred and twenty states do it, yes, but if we just say well France, Netherlands and Germany have done it and therefore everyone does it, I think that's a bit of a stretch.

SCHARF: So the thing about interpreting a statute, it's like interpreting the U.S. Constitution. Are we going to be strict constructionists or can we evolve with the times? Going back to Carsten. The Special Tribunal for Lebanon, which is another one of these international tribunals, had this precedent-setting decision on contempt. Can you tell us about that and why it might be relevant to the question that we're talking about and interpreting the ICC statute?

STAHN: Indeed, this was a very special decision of the Special Tribunal for Lebanon, who had to decide whether contempt of court could be exercised against a media company, and it's not in the statute in itself.[52] It just uses the term "persons"; it doesn't specify whether its natural or legal person. And it then found that corporate criminal responsibility is a general principle of law which is, of course, a very far-reaching statement.[53] If we look at it, this decision has been disputed. Some scholars have said this is wishful thinking, but we don't have enough evidence for it. Others have endorsed it, so I don't think first of all, it's only related to contempt powers. not to international crimes. Secondly, it was influenced by the fact that Lebanon has corporate criminal liability in its domestic code.[54] So that means I think we shouldn't overstretch the decision. It might have an important effect

50. *Id.*

51. *See Clifford Chance, Corporate Liability in Europe* (2012) https://www.cliffordchance.com/content/dam/cliffordchance/PDFs/Corporate_Liability_in_Europe.pdf.

52. *See* De Jonge, *International Corporate Criminal Liability at the Special Tribunal for Lebanon: Prosecutor v. Karma Al Khayat and Al Jadeed,* Palace Peace Library (May 8, 2015) https://www.peacepalacelibrary.nl/2015/05/ international-corporate-criminal-liability-at-the-special-tribunal-for-lebanon-prosecutor-v-karma-al-khayat-and-al-jadeed/.

53. *Id.*

54. *Id.*

in signaling like the ICC through a decision. You might trigger domestic reform, you might make NGOs think differently about the issue, and it's about the shadow of the law where this decision might be important.

SCHARF: Now assuming that the ICC prosecutor is going to be going against corporate officers for corporate actions, let's take a specific, concrete example and see how that might play out. Milena, let's talk about human trafficking. So what's that crime, what does it involve? Could it be a crime against humanity?

STERIO: So there's actually a definition of trafficking in the so-called Palermo Product Protocol, which is a protocol adopted as a supplementary protocol to the UN Convention against transnational organized crime. The Palermo Protocol defines trafficking in persons as the recruitment, transportation, transfer, harboring, or receipt of persons by means of the threat or use of force or other forms of coercion.[55] Now when it comes to prosecuting trafficking, arguably you could prosecute it as part of Article 7 of the Rome Statute of the ICC, which is the article on crimes against humanity and that article actually has a so-called trafficking clause in Article 7-1(c), which explicitly refers to trafficking in persons and in particular women and children.[56] Trafficking has been investigated and essentially prosecuted as part of crimes of sexual violence within the Yugoslavia and the Rwanda Tribunals, and it could be potentially prosecuted in the ICC. However, if it's prosecuted as a crime against humanity, it would have to take place on a widespread and systematic scale, like an attack against the civilian population and obviously, any time we talk about the ICC, as Carsten already identified, there are significant jurisdictional and admissible hurdles to any ICC prosecution.

SCHARF: So here is the thing about corporations: they're unlikely to be involved in prostitution per se or slave labor per se—well some of them might be—but they are more frequently going to be facilitating the trafficking. So let's talk to Tim Webster about a situation where a corporation creates a website that allows traffickers to advertise, let's say, the availability of child prostitutes. Could the corporation and its officers be liable for the actual trafficking simply by allowing them to advertise on their website?

---

55. Protocol to Prevent, Suppress and Punish Trafficking in Persons Especially Women and Children, supplementing the United Nations Convention against Transnational Organized Crime, Nov. 15, 2000, U.N.R 15/25.

56. Rome Statute of the International Criminal Court, art. 7, sc. 3, July 17, 1998 2187 U.N.T.S. 90 (entered into force July 1, 2002).

WEBSTER: I think the aiding and abetting decisions under Alien Tort have all been about corporations aiding and abetting governments, so this would be distinct from that. Here you're talking about one corporation, you know, helping another one set up a website, so that may pose some problems. On the other hand, as we talked about with *Kiobel*: if we can say that human trafficking is a part of international law, there was sufficiently crystallized customary international law, and it affects an important U.S. national interest. Then yes, I could certainly see the jurisdiction being allowed and the case moving forward. But, again, I haven't seen that case unfolding just yet.

SCHARF: So that's the website type of case. Tim, let's take a different scenario: what if a corporation purchases goods from a group that is involved in human trafficking? Could the corporation be criminally liable if it knew that it was getting those goods and they were being exploited by these laborers? So I'm thinking, for example, of corporations that purchase shrimp from the shrimp peeling shed operators in Thailand these—I don't know if you're familiar with this case, it's pretty horrific—but these people are paid almost nothing. They are migrant workers, they're almost enslaved there. Then other companies around the world, including many of our producers of shrimp, are just buying their shrimp, you know, with full knowledge of what's going on.[57] Could those companies be prosecuted for the human trafficking for their involvement in aiding and embedding?

WEBSTER: Yeah, that's a tough question. I would say, you know, we need to—if we're talking about criminal prosecution—we need to make sure that we have a clear statute on the book that a federal prosecutor can hang his hat on. I haven't heard of that particular case, and I suspect the reason is because federal prosecutors have enough to deal with when they're trying to handle U.S. domestic crimes. So they may feel that their resources are best targeted or best spent targeting issues that are of more central concern to the United States. Now that's not to say it's impossible; maybe if this does become a major issue, does try to love a media attention. But I just I can't see a state or federal prosecutor using those resources to prosecute shrimp production as opposed to human trafficking here in Ohio.

---

57. *See* Felicity Lawrence & Kate Hodal, *Thailand Accused of Failing to Stamp Out Murder and Slavery in Fishing Industry,* The Guardian (Mar. 30, 2017, 2:00 AM), https://www.the-guardian.com/global-development/2017/mar/30/thailand-failing-to-stamp-out-murder-slavery-fishing-industry-starvation-forced-labour-trafficking.

SCHARF: That's going to have to be the last word as we're running out of time. I think we learned a lot about the civil and criminal prospects for liability of corporations. Judge Buergenthal, Dean Sterio, Professors Cover and Webster and Carsten Stahn, thank you all for providing your insights on the liability of corporations for human rights abuses. I'm Michael Scharf, you've been listening to *Talking Foreign Policy.*

"Talking Foreign Policy" is a production of Case Western Reserve University and is produced in partnership with 90.3 FM WCPN ideastream. Questions and comments about the topics discussed on the show or to suggest future topics, email talkingforeignepolicy@case.edu.

Contributors

Ambassador Reuben Brigety is the dean of the Elliott School of International Affairs of The George Washington University. Prior to joining the Elliott School, he served as United States ambassador to the African Union and is a permanent representative to the United Nations Economic Commission for Africa.

Thomas Creely, PhD is director of the Ethics and Emerging Military Technology Graduate Program at the U.S. Naval War College and is adjunct professor at Brown University School of Professional Studies Executive Master in Cybersecurity.

Marian Wright Edelman is the 2017 recipient of the Inamori Ethics Prize, and the founder and president of the Washington, DC-based Children's Defense Fund (CDF), which grew out of the Civil Rights Movement.

Howard Ernst, PhD is professor of Political Science at the United States Naval Academy, where he teaches classes on the US political system and environmental security.

David J. Kritz, PhD is the program director of the Master of Science of Strategic Intelligence Program, Student Service advisor for Air Force Students, and an assistant professor at the National Intelligence University, where he manages the daily operations of the graduate program and teaches students Leadership and Management in the Intelligence Community, Thesis Methodology and Design, and Professional Ethics.

Crystal An, J. Lucas Hii, and Yash Kumar are undergraduate students or recent alumni at Case Western Reserve University and on the Executive Board of the Global Ethical Leaders Society (GELS).

J. Lucas Hii, Ellen Kendall, Jacob Sandstrom, Roston Shore, and Vanitha Raguveer are undergraduate students or recent alumni at Case Western Reserve University.

Michael Scharf, JD is co-dean of the Case Western Reserve University Law School, director of the Frederick K. Cox International Law Center, and host of *Talking Foreign Policy*.

Colonel James A. Schnell (USAF, retired), PhD is a collaborative expert in the Institute for Research & Development at Duy Tan University (Danang, Vietnam).